STAMP COLLECTING

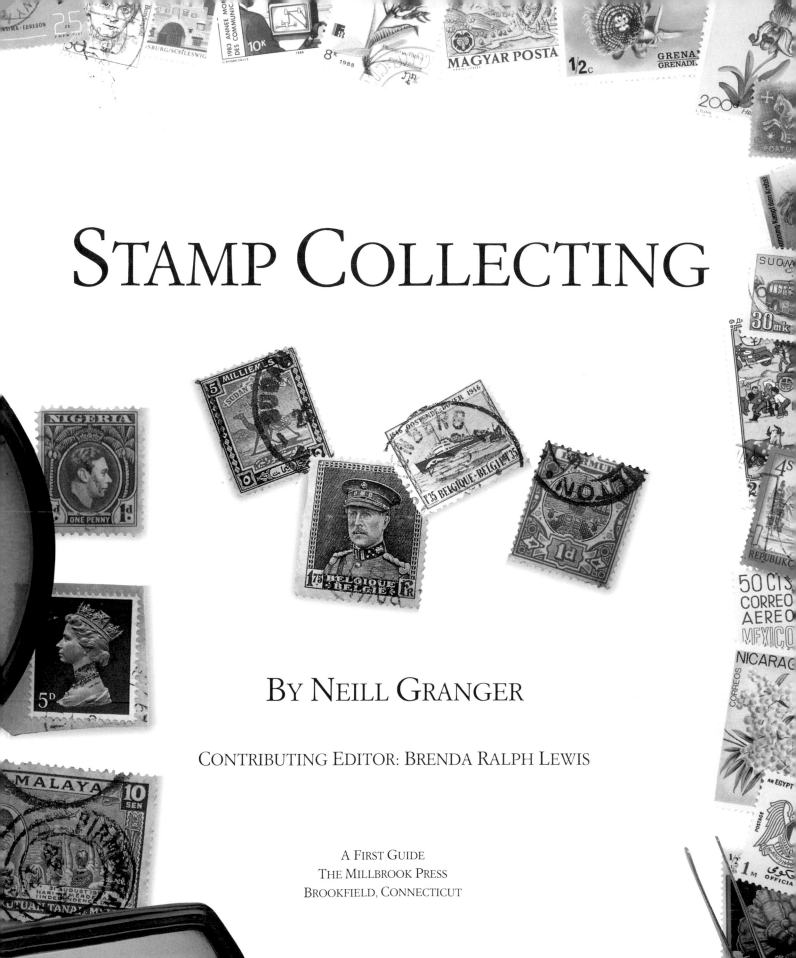

STAMP COLLECTING

BY NEILL GRANGER

CONTRIBUTING EDITOR: BRENDA RALPH LEWIS

A FIRST GUIDE
THE MILLBROOK PRESS
BROOKFIELD, CONNECTICUT

A QUARTO BOOK

First published in the United States of America in 1994 by
The Millbrook Press
2 Old New Milford Road
Brookfield, Connecticut 06804

Library of Congress Cataloging-in-Publication-Data

Granger, Neill.
    Stamp collecting / Neill Granger.
        p.   cm.
    Includes index.
    Summary: Young philatelists will learn about the invention of
stamps, what makes a stamp valuable, and what a collector should look
for when assembling a collection.
        ISBN 1-56294-734-6 (trade ed.). – ISBN 1-56294-399-5 (lib. ed.)
        1. Postage-stamps--Collectors and collecting--Juvenile literature.
    [1. Postage stamps--Collectors and collecting.]   I. Title.
    HE6203.G7   1994
    769.56--dc20   94-6390
                                                                              CIP
                                                                              AC

This book was designed and produced by
Quarto Children's Books Ltd.
The Fitzpatrick Building
188–194 York Way
London N7 9QP

Editors Jackie Dobbyne, Helen Varley
Designer Ian Hunt
Photographers Paul Forrester, Martin Norris
Illustrator Julian Baker

Quarto would like to give special thanks to Neill Granger and to Stanley
Gibbons Auctions Ltd. for providing the majority of stamps and covers in this
book. We would also like to acknowledge the assistance of Brenda Ralph Lewis
in supplying many stamps and covers from her private collection.

Picture Acknowledgments
Ace Photo Agency/Benelux Press, page 70al. Nigel Bradley, page 39acr, bl. Tony
Bray International Stamp Dealers, page 71br. Bridgeman Art Library, page 12ar.
British Airways, page 29b. Christie's Images, pages 11br, 29br. Dauwalder's of
Salisbury, page 15ar. Jackie Dobbyne, pages 39cl, 47cl, bl, br, 57ac, 60cl, 61cr,
b, 70ac, 71c, 77c, b, 86cl. Stanley Gibbons Ltd., pages 30al, 32ar, 51bl, 55bl, r.
Harmer's of London, pages 31cl, 32cl, cr, 33ar. H R Harmer Inc., New York,
page 31c. Hulton-Deutsch Collection, pages 26a, 27ar, 31al, 66br. Harrison and
Sons Ltd., page 18b. Illustrated London News Picture Library, page 13b.
Mansell Collection, page 31ac. Will Payne, pages 33cl, b. Popperfoto, page 41ar.
By courtesy of the Post Office, pages 12bl, 13al, 14al, 26cl, 26–27b, 27cr, 38ac,
55ar, 85ar. Bernard Stonehouse, pages 82cl, r, 83a, c. Trip, pages 34b, 60ac,
61ac, 71bl. United Airlines, page 29a. Kenneth Wenger, page 62bl. Trevor
Wood, page 19cr.
Quarto Publishing would like to thank the above for supplying photographs and
for permission to reproduce copyright material. While every effort has been
made to trace and acknowledge all copyright holders, we would like to apologize
should any omissions have been made.

Typeset by Central Southern Typesetters, Eastbourne, Sussex
Manufactured by Eray Scan (Pte.) Ltd., Singapore
Printed by Star Standard Industries (Pte.) Ltd., Singapore

CONTENTS

ALL ABOUT STAMPS

Stamps are a window on the world. They can tell you about a country's history, geography, politics, and economy; its great achievements and its famous citizens; its fashions and its culture. There are many thousands of stamps to collect and many different ways to do so. In this book, you'll learn all about stamps and discover how to make your collection unique.

RECORD-BREAKING STAMPS

RAREST IN THE WORLD
BRITISH GUIANA 1856 ONE-CENT BLACK ON MAGENTA
This stamp, of which there is only one in the world, was sold for $935,000 in 1980. (See also page 28.)

FIRST
GREAT BRITAIN 1840 PENNY BLACK
This was the first stamp ever issued, on May 6, 1840. (See also page 14.)

MOST VALUABLE
ONE PENNY RED AND TWO PENCE BLUE "POST OFFICE" MAURITIUS COVER 1847
This cover was sold in 1993 for five million Swiss francs. It is the most valuable cover in the world. (See also page 31.)

MOST UNUSUAL
BHUTAN 1973 PLAYING RECORD
This plastic stamp is one of a set of seven issued in 1973 that play the national anthem (in English or Bhutanese), local folk songs, or give a talk about the history of Bhutan.

FIRST TRAPEZOID
MALAYSIA 1967 30 CENTS
This stamp was issued on December 2, 1967, to commemorate the centenary of the first stamps issued by the Straits Settlements.

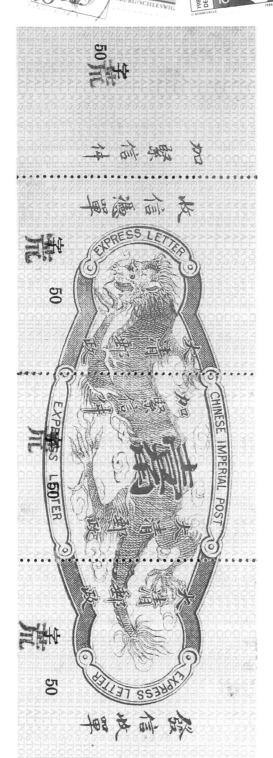

LARGEST

CHINA 1913 10-CENT EXPRESS LABEL
This measures 9¾ x 2¾ inches
(248 x 70 mm). It is divided into
four parts. Only the third part (the
dragon's body) was used as a stamp.

STRANGEST SHAPE

NORFOLK ISLAND 1974
10 CENTS
This stamp, which commemorates the
centenary of the Universal Postal
Union, is in the shape of the island.

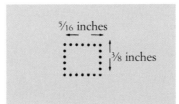

FIRST SELF-ADHESIVE

SIERRA LEONE 1964
This stamp is one of a set of 14 that
were also the first free-form stamps.
It is shaped like a map of the country.
(See also page 35.)

HIGHEST FACE VALUE

KENYA AND UGANDA 1925 £100
This "fiscal stamp" was used to pay
duty or taxes; it could also serve as a
postage stamp, but rarely did so due to
its high value. In the 1940s the U.S.
issued fiscal stamps with a face value of
$10,000, which were only valid for
collecting revenue.

RAREST IN EUROPE

SWEDEN 1855 3 SKILLING-BANCO
This is the only known example of the
3-skilling stamp in the yellow color
instead of the usual green. It is worth a
fortune. (See also page 28.)

SMALLEST

By comparison, the smallest stamp in
the world, the 1863–66 10 centavos
and one peso from the Colombian
state of Bolivar, measures only ⁵⁄₁₆ x ³⁄₈
inches (8 x 9.5 mm). The box above
shows the tiny shape.

⁵⁄₁₆ inches
³⁄₈ inches

FIRST TRIANGULAR

CAPE OF GOOD HOPE 1853
FOUR PENCE
This stamp was issued on
September 1, 1853.

THE FIRST LETTER CARRIERS

People have always needed to communicate with one another. As ancient civilizations developed, reliable methods of communication became increasingly important. There were messenger services in ancient Egypt from 1580 BC, and throughout the Assyrian Empire after 671 BC. However, the first system to resemble our modern postal service was that of King Darius of Persia and his successors between 550 BC and 333 BC. From the Mediterranean to India, there were relay stations along the roads between important cities for the swift transfer of men and horses to carry messages throughout the empire.

The very first letters were written on clay tablets like this Assyrian one.

CURSUS PUBLICUS

The Persian communication system was improved by the Romans. Two systems were used by the *Cursus Publicus*, the Roman post office, along the excellent Roman roads: the *cursus velox* – the express route for letters using horses or wheeled carts, and the *cursus clabularis* used to transport food and military supplies.

Before postal systems developed, a messenger would carry just one letter. This method was too expensive for most people.

PRIVATE POST

Postal systems then collapsed for 600 years until Marco Polo, in the thirteenth century in China, established a network of relay stations using 300,000 horses. Meanwhile, in Europe, from the end of the thirteenth century, commerce, education, and town life were developing.

Merchants, monasteries, and universities established private postal systems that continued until the late fifteenth and early sixteenth centuries when the European monarchs established their own communication systems.

These Swiss stamps show letter carriers of the past.

POSTAL HORN

In the Middle Ages in Europe, trades guilds organized the first international postal service. The Metzger Post organized by the butchers' guild, like many later postal services, used a curved horn to announce the mail (right). Since then, a postal horn has been featured as an emblem for many national postal services.

MESSAGE FOR THE EMPEROR

In ancient Peru, *chasquis,* or messengers (left), used to run along the mountain roads to deliver messages for the *Sapa Inca*, the emperor.

NEAT AND CLEAN

Before postage stamps were invented, envelopes were not used for letters. Messages were written on one side of a sheet of paper only and when the letter was finished, all the sheets were folded in half with the message on one side and the other side left clean for the address. The sheets were folded twice more to make two flaps and one was tucked into the other. This kept the letter neat and clean on its journey. If more than one sheet of paper was used, the outside sheet bearing the address was called the "wrapper."

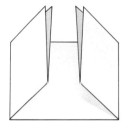

Fold in half.

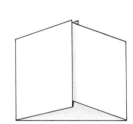

Fold the ends to make flaps.   Tuck one flap into the other.

THE DAKS OF INDIA

The *dak* runners of India carried letters in a cleft stick, accompanied by a *mashalchi,* or torch-bearer, to light the way at night and a tom-tom beater to ward off wild animals. The dak system was most widespread during the sixteenth century when 4,000 runners were used, but in some remote areas, dak runners are still used today.

Horse daks were introduced in 1541 on the 2,000-mile (3,220-km) route between Bengal and Sind. Mail carts, known as *dak tonga* (right), were introduced in the eighteenth century.

A Penny to Go Anywhere

The first postage stamp was issued by Great Britain on May 6, 1840. It was called the Penny Black and was introduced after a former schoolteacher, Rowland Hill, suggested a simple, efficient, and inexpensive postal service.

Before prepaid stamps, the cost of postage was worked out by the number of sheets of paper in a letter and the distance the letter had to travel. Postage was expensive and had to be paid by the person who received the letter, who often refused to hand over the money. In fact, the use of coded addresses meant that sometimes the contents of a letter could be understood without being opened and the letter returned to the postman. Naturally, this upset the Post Office. Once Rowland Hill suggested the stamp and a standard penny rate was introduced, postage could be paid in advance, ensuring income for the Post Office. It also meant that the postal service was no longer only available to companies or to the rich. Stamps proved to be such a good idea that soon the rest of the world took up the idea.

This Victorian balance was used for weighing letters between 1840 and 1870.

SIR ROWLAND HILL

ECOLE DE PHILATELIE
CHARLEROI 1960-1965
SCHOOL DER PHILATELIE

THE FIRST STAMPS
This timeline shows when countries first issued stamps.

POST OFFICE MAURITIUS
This stamp, issued on September 21, 1847, was hand engraved by a half-blind local watchmaker. Instead of saying "Post Paid Mauritius" the stamps had "Post Office Mauritius" written on them by mistake. Only 500 copies of each value were printed, so very few exist today.

GREAT BRITAIN PENNY BLACK
This was the first stamp ever printed. It is a well known stamp but it is not rare. There were over 68 million Penny Blacks issued.

1840	1841	1842	1843	1844	1845	1846	1847	1848	1849	1850	1851

BRAZIL "BULL'S EYE"
This stamp was issued on August 1, 1843. It is famous because Brazil was the second country to issue stamps. It earned its nickname because its shape is similar to a bull's eye.

U.S.A. FIVE CENTS AND TEN CENTS
The first stamps issued by the United States, on July 1, 1847, featured Benjamin Franklin, the first U.S. postmaster general, and George Washington, the first president (right.)

This Belgian first day cover features Sir Rowland Hill, inventor of the prepaid stamp.

F.D.C.
P. 156

CRISS-CROSS LETTERS

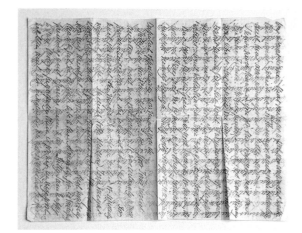

It cost a lot of money to send a letter overseas, so people wrote on every available space on the sheet. Sometimes, people wrote twice on the same side. When a page was full, they would turn the sheet 90 degrees and start again across the first lines.

NAPLES ½ TORNESO
Naples was still a separate kingdom when it issued its first stamp in 1858. Two years later, Naples joined with the other states to form a unified country, Italy, which issued its first stamp in 1862.

CAPE OF GOOD HOPE TRIANGULAR
This, the first odd-shaped stamp, was issued in 1853.

| 852 | 1853 | 1854 | 1855 | 1856 | 1857 | 1858 | 1859 | 1860 |

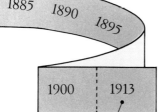

1870 1875 1880 1885 1890 1895

| 1900 | 1913 |

BRITISH GUIANA COTTON REELS
These stamps, first issued on July 1, 1850, were printed in a local newspaper office. They are called cotton reels because the rough, round design on the stamps looks like the label on a reel (spool) of cotton thread.

FINLAND FIVE KOPEKS
The currency on the first Finnish stamp was kopeks, the currency of Russia, since Finland was still a part of Russia in 1856.

AUSTRALIA £2
The states that make up Australia did not join together until 1911, so its first Commonwealth stamps were not issued until 1913.

ANATOMY OF A STAMP

Every stamp tells a story. By looking carefully at a stamp, you may be able to discover which country issued it and when; its value; whether it is a definitive, commemorative, or special stamp; how it was printed; and how it was perforated.

REASON FOR ISSUE
Commemorative stamps are issued to mark an anniversary or special event. This stamp commemorates the 25th annual Stamp Day in Italy.

THREE MAIN GROUPS
Every stamp belongs to one of three main classifications:

DEFINITIVE STAMPS
These are the everyday stamps always available at the post office (right). They range in value from the smallest unit of currency to high values for heavy packages.

COMMEMORATIVE STAMPS
These are issued on their own or in sets to mark an anniversary or special event (left).

SPECIAL STAMPS
Larger than definitive stamps, these are issued to depict the life of a country – its animals, buildings, scenery, and so on. (Some collectors call any decorative stamp a commemorative.)

PRINTER
The name of the printer is sometimes shown on the stamp. More information about the printer may be found in a stamp catalogue.

YEAR OF ISSUE
Many countries now include the year of issue. Knowing the date makes it easier to find the stamp in a catalogue and helps you to arrange the stamp in the right order in your collection.

PERFORATIONS
These are the holes between the stamps on the sheet.

POSTMARK
The postmark shows when and where this stamp was posted.

R. RIZZI

COUNTRY NAME
Every country in the world, except Great Britain, has to include its name on stamps. Great Britain is the exception because it was the first country to issue stamps. Look on pages 88 and 89 if you do not know the English name of the country on a stamp.

FACE VALUE
This is the price of the stamp. It is usually printed in figures, often with the currency name in letters.

DESIGNER
Some stamps include the name of the designer or artist.

CUT OR TEAR?

The first stamps did not have perforations and are now known as imperforates. They had to be cut from the sheet using scissors. Because this was very inconvenient, manufacturers began experimenting with machines to make perforations around the stamps. Older stamps were perforated after printing. Today, printing and perforating is sometimes done in a continuous operation.

SCISSORS OUT
This Greek stamp of 1861 (right) is imperforate. Some countries still make imperforate stamps.

LINE BY LINE
Line perforations make vertical and horizontal lines in two operations so the holes at the corners do not perfectly match (right).

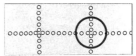

Line perforation

ALL TOGETHER NOW
Comb perforations are made by a machine that looks like a comb with very few teeth. It perforates one row of stamps at a time. Here the holes at the corners of the stamps match perfectly (right).

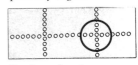

Comb perforation

EARLY EFFORTS

ROULETTES
Roulettes are made by making cuts between the stamps, without removing any paper. These cuts are usually short lines with gaps in between. This method is not used very often today.

SNAKY STAMPS
Early stamps, like these from Finland, had unusual, snake-like perforations that were known as serpentines.

HOW A STAMP IS MADE

When a new stamp is required, perhaps to commemorate Christmas or a new president, a committee usually decides on the subject or theme for the stamp or set of stamps. Several artists are invited to submit designs, and the committee selects the best of these. The illustration for the stamp may be drawn, painted, or photographed. It is often much larger than life-size. When the illustration is finished and approved, lettering is added and the artwork is sent to the printer.

The printer sends a sample or proof to be checked carefully against the original design. Any mistakes in color, lettering, or register (the correct alignment of colors and lines) must be corrected by the printer. Once the proof is approved, millions of stamps are printed on long rolls of paper. These are cut into sheets and perforated before more careful checking, to make sure no mistakes have occurred.

Stamp collectors are delighted to find errors, as this often makes stamps more valuable, but printers try very hard to eliminate them all. Once counted, the new stamps are ready to be sold to the public.

Here is the famous children's book illustrator, Quentin Blake (above), working on his design, and the finished stamp (top right).

A printer corrects blemishes in the tiny reproductions of a stamp design on the curved copper photogravure printing cylinder (top) and (right) a printer checks proofs hot off the press. Printed stamps are sorted, checked, and packed (above).

JOINED TOGETHER

Many countries issue stamps of two or more individual designs joined together. These are known as se tenant stamps. Examples include this 1976 Swedish pair (below right) illustrating the countryside and fishing. Usually, se tenant stamps have a common theme. This U.S. set honored the 100th anniversary of the American Museum of Natural History in New York City.

PAPER PATTERNS

A watermark is a pattern pressed into the paper when it is made to make it more difficult to forge stamps. Printing techniques today are very sophisticated so watermarks are not always necessary.

This 1963 San Marino stamp has a "three feathers" watermark which can just be seen when it is held up to the light.

The light areas in the watermark are places where the paper is slightly thinner, and more light comes through.

JIGSAW STAMPS

Where the different designs in a series of stamps make a complete picture, the set is called a composite design. Each of the stamps in this 1967 U.S. set (right) depicting a decade of achievement in space makes a picture, but each pair fits together like two jigsaw pieces to make a composite design.

UPSIDE DOWN

Sometimes stamps are issued with one row upside down as in this example of South African stamps (far left). This is usually done for booklets. The Cape of Good Hope triangular stamps (left) were printed this way to save paper. Stamps printed upside down are described as tête-bêche.

AT THE PRINTER'S

Recess, typography, photogravure, and offset lithography. These are the names of the four main printing processes. Each one is very different. If you look carefully, you can tell how the stamps in your collection were printed.

RECESS PRINTING

Rub the stamp gently. If you can feel raised lines, it was probably recess printed.

In recess printing, the design of the stamp is made up of many fine lines. These lines are cut into a metal printing plate and ink is forced into them. The printing plate is then pressed on to a sheet of paper to print the stamps. The ink sits slightly above the surface of the paper so the stamp may feel a little rough if you rub it gently.

Recess printing, also known as line engraving or intaglio, was used to print the Penny Black and other early stamps. It is still used today.

These stamps from Southern Rhodesia (top) and Monaco (above) were recess printed.

TYPOGRAPHY

Look at the back of the stamp. Tiny ridges are a clue to a stamp printed by typography.

Typography is the opposite of recess printing. Here the series of fine lines that make up the design is built up on to the surface of the plate. The raised design takes the ink from inked rollers, then transfers it to the paper. If you look at the back of an unused stamp printed this way, you may be able to see tiny ridges where the design has been pressed on to the paper.

Typography, also known as letterpress, is a cheaper and faster method than recess printing. It was used to produce many stamps between 1860 and 1930.

These stamps issued by the Straits Settlements (top) and France (above) were printed by typography.

Use a magnifying glass to study your stamps. You should be able to spot the clues that show what printing method was used.

PHOTOGRAVURE

Look at the edges of the letters and shapes on the stamp. If the edges of the letters are ragged, the stamp was probably printed by photogravure.

Photogravure, a modern version of recess printing, was first used in 1914. Each color used in the design is photographed through a very fine screen. This breaks down the picture into tiny dots. The photograph is then etched on to a printing cylinder, a different one for each color, to make a series of fine hollows. The printing ink is forced into the hollows before being transferred to the paper. If you use a magnifying glass, you can usually tell stamps that have been printed by photogravure because the small colored dots make the edges of letters and figures appear ragged.

These Belgian (top) and Dutch (left) stamps were printed by photogravure.

OFFSET LITHOGRAPHY

Through your magnifying glass, the edges of stamps printed by offset look quite smooth.

Offset lithography, or simply offset, is based on the principle that water and grease do not mix. The printing plates are made in a similar way to photogravure but the design of the stamp is made from material that repels water. When the printing plate is wetted before it is inked, the pattern remains dry. It therefore collects the greasy printing ink and transfers it to the paper. Combinations of four colors are used for most designs. Stamps printed by offset have much neater edges than those printed by photogravure. Most stamps today are printed by offset.

These Maltese (top) and Swiss (right) stamps were printed by offset.

FOUR-COLOR PRINTING

The whole range of colors can be made by combinations of the four printing colors, cyan (blue), yellow, magenta (red), and black. The process can be seen in this miniature sheet from Barbados. First, the cyan plate is printed (1). Then the yellow plate is printed (2). Next, the magenta plate is printed. In this example, magenta is shown printed on its own (3), and with yellow (4). Finally, the black plate is printed (5). The finished stamp shows the effect of all four colors printed together (6).

MIXED DOUBLES

Sometimes a combination of printing processes is used. On this Belgian stamp, recess printing has been used for the finely etched detail and photogravure to add some color to the background.

Photogravure printing

Recess printing

SPOT THE MISTAKE!

Stamp collectors are delighted if they can find a mistake, as this can make a stamp rare and valuable. Generally, design errors are not valuable unless the mistake is noticed and corrected after only a few stamps are printed, but it can be interesting to have examples of both the error and the corrected design in a collection. Here are some of the most common mistakes.

MISSING COLORS
Sometimes the printing machine runs out of one color, or it stops printing properly. These mistakes are spectacular but they do not happen often, so stamps with missing colors are rare and expensive. This Bermuda 1962 3d error (left, below) is worth nearly 7,000 times more than the correct one (above).

DOUBLE PERFORATIONS
Older perforating machines stamped out perforations one row at a time. If the machine stopped and started again, a row of stamps would have two sets of perforations, as in this corner block of 1953 British definitive 1 shilling stamps (below). The "teeth" of the comb perforator are clearly shown.

CONSTANT VARIETIES
These are small marks that are transferred from the printing cylinder to all the sheets of stamps. Some of these constant varieties are interesting and may make a good addition to your collection. Very small marks are called "fly specks."

INVERTED PRINTING
The colors of older stamps were printed one at a time. If a sheet of stamps was put into the machine upside down, then that color would be inverted. This happened with the 1962 issue of a U.S. stamp (right and below) featuring Dag Hammarskjold, who was secretary-general of the United Nations from 1953 to 1961. The stamps had already been issued when the error was spotted. More were printed so that the variety would not be valuable. Today, the printing process is continuous so this kind of mistake cannot occur

OFFSET ON REVERSE
This is the stamp collector's term for stamps which have stuck together after printing and before the gum and ink are dry. The picture from one sheet of stamps is marked on the gummed back of the sheet that is placed on top. The design is reversed just the same as if you drew a picture with felt-tip pens and laid a sheet of paper on top.

"OH DEAR!"

For most collectors, the most amusing mistakes are design errors. These are mistakes made by the artist who draws the picture that is used for the stamps. Of course, there can be all sorts of mistakes of this type. Place names may be spelled incorrectly when they are part of the drawing, or people's titles misidentified. Sometimes a detail in the drawing may be missed. And sometimes a detail may be added. Take a look at these funny mistakes.

On the 1938 Fiji stamp shown on the left, the artist has forgotten to put a man in the boat.

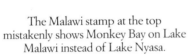

The Malawi stamp at the top mistakenly shows Monkey Bay on Lake Malawi instead of Lake Nyasa.

This Norfolk Island stamp on the left says Governor Philip is meeting the Home Society instead of the Home Secretary.

On the 1956 stamp from the former East Germany on the left, the illustration of composer Robert Schumann shows music by Franz Schubert.

This 1903 stamp from St. Kitts-Nevis shows Christopher Columbus using a telescope one hundred years before it was invented!

A Stamp's Journey

Millions of letters and packages are mailed every day, and most arrive safely at the correct destination. This is because modern postal systems all over the world are well organized and highly mechanized. Much of the work of sorting and canceling is done by machines that can work efficiently all day and all night. This series of U.S. stamps shows a stamp's journey in the mail from purchase at the post office to delivery by the postal worker.

1 Stamps are usually bought from a post office, either torn from a perforated sheet or sold in a booklet.

The stamp should be stuck on the top right corner of the envelope. This makes sure that the sorting machine will get the envelope the right way to "read" the address.

U.S. POSTAL SERVICE 8¢

U.S. POSTAL SERVICE 8¢

5 The machines sort and cancel (1) the stamps so they cannot be used again. Large envelopes and those with the stamps in the wrong place have to be canceled by hand.

If there is a zip code on a letter, a special machine types it in phosphor on the envelope in a series of dots or dashes (2) that the automatic sorting machines can "read." All the envelopes are then sorted into different bundles to be sent on to the next destination.

6 Depending on how far the bags of mail have to travel, they may be sent by truck, by railroad, or by plane. A letter may pass through several sorting offices before it reaches the town to which it has been addressed.

2 Once it has a stamp on it, the letter can be mailed.

3 A post office worker collects the mail from the mailbox at regular intervals during the day. Collection times are displayed on the front of the mailbox.

4 All the mailbags are taken to the sorting office in the nearest large town. They are emptied out and the letters sent through sorting machines.

7 Once there, it will be sorted again into streets and put in a pigeon hole ready to be delivered to homes and offices by a postal worker.

8 By the time a letter reaches its destination, its envelope can tell you where it was mailed (1), when it was collected (2), and at what time it began its journey through the mail (3).

THE MAIL MUST GET THROUGH!

Delivering the mail hasn't always been as straightforward as it is today!

UNDER PRESSURE
In Austria, France, Germany, Great Britain, and Italy, a pneumatic postal service operated in the late 1800s. Mail was placed in special containers and sent at high speed by air pressure through tubes underground (below).

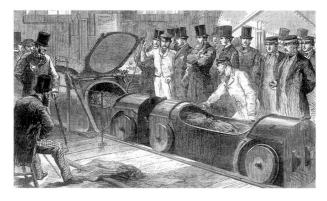

"ALL ABOARD!"
During the nineteenth century, the network of railways across Europe grew, and, since trains were faster and more reliable than stagecoaches, these were used to carry mail. By the second half of the century, the mail was sorted on board, saving additional time. Look out for Traveling Post Office (TPO) cancels.

This 1984 French stamp shows a French train on which mail is sorted.

HORSE POWER
In Europe, North America, and Australia during the late nineteenth century, stagecoaches were used to carry mail (above). They were pulled by horses, and journeys took a long time, as there were many stops to change the tired animals. In North America, urgent mail was carried by riders on horseback, the famous Pony Express.

FIRST FLIGHTS
By the 1930s, airplanes carried letters between countries all over the world (below). About the same time, the great German airships (far right) were also used to carry mail.

This 1965 Italian stamp commemorates the night air mail service.

In remote areas, more unusual ways to collect and deliver the mail were developed.

WHATEVER THE WEATHER

In the hot, dry center of Australia, bicycles and camels were used to carry the mail to remote mining communities. Camels were also used in Egypt and the Sudan (right). During the long, bitter winters in Russia and Scandinavia, horses and reindeer pulled sleighs over the snow and ice. In India, bullock-drawn carts were used between 1846 and 1904.

SHARK ATTACK!

Remote islands have come up with elaborate postal systems. In the seventeenth century, mail from Ascension Island in the Atlantic Ocean was left in glass bottles on rocks, and collected by small boats from passing ships. The Tin Can Mail Service in Tonga, in the Pacific Ocean, worked in the same way. It began in 1882 when a swimmer carrying letters out to a ship was killed by a shark!

The islanders of Samoa and many other small islands in the Pacific Ocean used rafts to collect their mail because it was too dangerous for ships to come into the shore. Later, seaplanes collected and delivered mail (above).

UNDER SIEGE

During the Franco-Prussian war between France and Prussia (1870–1871), Paris was surrounded by the enemy. There were several experiments to get mail out of Paris. The most dramatic used a hot-air balloon. Over 50 flights were successful.

Mail that had to be brought into the city was placed in watertight zinc balls, called *boules de moulin*, which were floated on the Seine River (right).

FINGERS CROSSED

The remote Scottish island of St. Kilda had a most unusual mail service that depended largely on luck! Islanders placed letters in hollowed-out driftwood sealed in inflated sheep's bladders before tossing the package into the Atlantic Ocean (left). Eventually, the current washed the package up on to the shore of the mainland. This system was used until 1930 when the island was evacuated and became a bird sanctuary.

TABBY MAIL

In Liège, in Belgium, in 1879, 37 cats were used to carry bundles of letters within a 18.6-mile (30-km) radius of the city. The experiment was abandoned as the cats proved to be thoroughly undisciplined!

SPECIAL STAMPS

There are all sorts of special stamps: famous stamps, forged stamps, unusual stamps, non-postage stamps, stamps that have special postmarks, and stamps on special covers. This section will tell you all about some of the special stamps you might read about, and some that you might be lucky enough to find and add to your collection.

Stamps become famous for different reasons. Apart from the Penny Black, which almost everybody has heard of, most famous stamps are either very valuable or have an unusual feature. Here are some of the most famous:

BRITISH GUIANA ONE-CENT BLACK ON MAGENTA

Issued in 1856, this stamp was found by a schoolboy in British Guiana in 1873. It was eventually bought by Alfred Hind, an American millionaire collector, and sold in New York for $935,000.

GREAT BRITAIN 6D IR OFFICIAL

The "IR OFFICIAL" mark makes this Great Britain's rarest stamp. At one time, the Inland Revenue (similar to the U.S. Internal Revenue Service) used ordinary stamps with special overprints on all the sheets. The stamp shown was issued on May 14, 1905, the last day official stamps were used.

SWEDEN 3 SKILLING-BANCO

Skilling-banco was the Swedish currency used when this stamp was issued in 1855 in the yellow color of the 8-skilling stamp instead of the correct green of the 3-skilling stamp.

The stamp was discovered by a Stockholm schoolboy in 1885 on one of his father's old letters. He took it to a stamp dealer who paid the price he offered for a normal stamp. This is the only known example of this error and the stamp is now worth a fortune.

WESTERN AUSTRALIA INVERTED SWAN

This stamp looks as though the swan is upside down. In fact, it is the frame and the words "four pence" that are upside down. Only 14 stamps of this type have been discovered.

The first airmail services
started in September 1911.
The U.S.A. (above), Britain,
Denmark, and Italy all began
services at this time.

U.S. 1918 CURTISS JENNY 24 CENTS
This stamp is famous because the
biplane in the center of the design has
been printed upside down. Since only
100 stamps with this error were
printed, these stamps are both rare and
very valuable. One was sold at auction
for $135,000 in 1979. It is thc first of
many stamps commemorating the U.S.
airmail service.

FAMOUS COLLECTORS

Stamp collecting is often called "the king of hobbies." It's certainly the hobby of kings. King George V of England and his son King George VI were both enthusiastic collectors as are King Hussein of Jordan and Prince Rainier of Monaco. Many rich men have also been stamp collectors, and have been very determined in their efforts to buy rare and precious stamps.

Stanley Gibbons.

A BAG OF FORTUNE

One of the first collectors was Stanley Gibbons (1840–1913), who later became a world famous stamp dealer. In 1863, soon after he first started to sell stamps in Plymouth, England, Stanley Gibbons was offered a bag full of stamps by two sailors who had won them in a raffle. The bags were full of triangular stamps from the Cape of Good Hope in South Africa and he paid £5 for them. They would be worth millions today.

The Strand, near the Thames River in London, where Stanley Gibbons opened a shop (above), is still a center for stamp dealers.

This stamp featuring Philippe von Ferrary is one example from a Liechtenstein issue commemorating famous stamp collectors.

A LOT OF POCKET MONEY

Philippe von Ferrary (1848–1917), a very rich man who lived in Paris, began collecting stamps when he was ten years old. Later, he traveled all over Europe to attend stamp auctions and bought many expensive stamps, sometimes spending up to £2,000 per week on them. By the time he was thirty, von Ferrary owned the most complete collection of stamps known at the time. Von Ferrary's collection was sold after his death in 1917. His rare British Guiana one-cent black on magenta was bought by Alfred Hind, a British-born American millionaire. Hind thought he owned the only one. It is said that when he discovered a second copy, he bought it and burned it to make sure he owned a unique stamp.

THE FIRST COLLECTORS

The Penny Black, first issued 1840.

One of the first collectors of stamps was John Tomlynson, who began collecting on May 7, 1840, the day after the Penny Black was issued. Another early collector was an unknown young lady who placed an advertisement in *The Times* in 1841 requesting readers to send her their stamps. At this time, there were only three stamps to collect: the Penny Black, the Twopenny Blue, and the Penny Red. Early collectors were only interested in collecting as many copies of a stamp as possible.

The Penny Red, first issued 1841.

PEACE IN WAR

Philately, the name given to the study of stamps and postal methods, is a hobby that has appealed to royalty and presidents. Both King George VI of Great Britain and U.S. President Franklin Roosevelt found studying their stamps relaxing during the stressful times of the Second World War.

U.S. President Franklin Roosevelt (above and far right) was given rare Russian stamps by Josef Stalin, his wartime ally and U.S.S.R. Head of State. The Nazis issued forgeries of British stamps – with Stalin's head in place of Queen Elizabeth the Queen Mother, for example, on the 1937 Coronation stamp – as propaganda.

Alfred Hind (1856–1933) began collecting stamps in about 1891 and had the best collection of American stamps in his time. He also owned some of the world's rarest stamps – in addition to the British Guiana one-cent, he owned the only cover on which the famous Post Office Mauritius penny red and twopence blue stamps were used together.

ONLY THE BEST

The first job of Alfred H. Caspary (above), who died in 1955, was as a messenger on Wall Street in New York. Eventually, he became a prominent member of the New York Stock Exchange and one of the world's most famous stamp collectors. His motto was "nothing but the best," and his collection included a mint block of four Post Office Mauritius one penny stamps.

Maurice Burrus (1882–1959) was another rich and famous early collector. He was born in France and made his fortune in his family's tobacco business. His particular treasures were the cover bearing the one penny and twopence Post Office Mauritius previously owned by Alfred Hind, and the unique Perot Provisional stamp on cover once owned by Philippe von Ferrary.

FAMOUS FORGERS

This 1863–71 Hong Kong 96-cents stamp is an example of the work of Juan de Sperati.

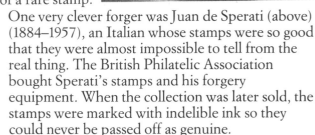

Real or fake? Sometimes, it's hard to tell because forgeries – that is, illegal copies – of stamps have been made to trick collectors, who will pay enormous sums of money for a rare stamp.

MASTER CRAFTSMAN
Really clever forgers were careful and not too greedy. To avoid collectors becoming suspicious, they did not make too many copies of a rare stamp.

One very clever forger was Juan de Sperati (above) (1884–1957), an Italian whose stamps were so good that they were almost impossible to tell from the real thing. The British Philatelic Association bought Sperati's stamps and his forgery equipment. When the collection was later sold, the stamps were marked with indelible ink so they could never be passed off as genuine.

This small printing machine is typical of those used by forgers in the nineteenth century.

All forgery equipment was on a small scale, even the perforating machines (above).

SILK PURSE FROM A SOW'S EAR
Sperati used ordinary, cheap stamps as a basis for making copies of rare ones. He used bleach to remove the color, then printed the forgery. In this way, the watermark, perforations, and postmark were absolutely correct.

FORGERY FACTORY
Sperati worked at a time when collectors who could not afford to buy rare stamps bought copies of them instead. Some of these copies had "facsimile" written on the back. The Spiro brothers, from Hamburg, Germany, used to mass-produce facsimiles. In order to avoid being accused of cheating the Post Office, Spiro forgeries were usually postmarked. So the poor stamp collector was cheated instead! Some of the many thousands of stamps the brothers made can still be found in old collections.

FOR ART'S SAKE?
François Fournier (1846–1927), a Swiss forger, called his facsimile stamps *objets d'art* because he thought they were works of art, not simply a way of making money. Nonetheless, thousands of Fournier's forgeries were sold as genuine stamps.

Fournier's work, like Sperati's, was considered so dangerous that, after his death in 1927, the Philatelic Society of Geneva bought his equipment and destroyed it.

Fournier also forged cheap stamps like this 1864 one real red of Mexico. A genuine copy of this stamp costs only a few pennies but by forging many copies Fournier could still make a lot of money.

FORGERY AT THE STOCK EXCHANGE!

Ordinary stamps have also been made to cheat post offices because the money paid for these stamps goes to the forger.

Between 1872 and 1874, a clerk at the Stock Exchange in London used forged 1867 one-shilling stamps on telegraph forms, stealing the genuine stamps and later selling them. At the time, one shilling was a lot of money. The forgeries were not discovered for 26 years and the clerk's identity remains a mystery.

Luckily, many forgeries are bad copies and can be easily detected.

PROPAGANDA!

Sometimes, forged stamps are meant not to deceive but to spread a message. This was particularly common during wartime for propaganda purposes.

During the Second World War (1939–1945) between Great Britain and the Commonwealth, France, the United States, the Soviet Union, and China (known as the Allies) on one side, and Germany, Italy, and Japan (called the Axis countries) on the other, both sides were skillful at producing propaganda forgeries.

The U.S. produced a stamp which cleverly altered a 1941 German stamp to show part of Adolf Hitler's face as a skull (above left). This, together with the words *Futsches Reich* meaning "Finished Empire" instead of *Deutsches Reich* (above right) meaning "German Empire," was intended to demoralize the German people and make them want to stop fighting.

This Italian stamp (right) shows Hitler and Benito Mussolini with the caption "Two peoples, one war". The Allies made this propaganda forgery (below centre) showing Hitler snarling at a startled Mussolini which reads "Two peoples, one leader." This was intended to suggest that Mussolini was frightened of and ruled by Hitler.

THE RIGHT TOOL FOR THE JOB

Some stamps are separated with cuts called "roulettes" instead of perforations. Roulettes are made by slitting the paper rather than removing part of it. Forgers had a marvelous collection of tools to make various kinds of roulettes – serpentine, sawtooth, arc, lozenge, and pin are names for some of them. Look at these examples:

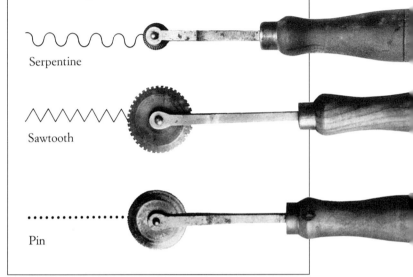

Serpentine

Sawtooth

Pin

The propaganda wasn't all one-sided though. The British Silver Jubilee stamp of 1935 (below right) was altered to show Stalin in place of George V, with the inscription "This war is a Jewsh [*sic*] war" and the Communist symbol of a hammer and sickle (bottom right). Germany hoped that if the British people suffering hardship felt that they were fighting on behalf of Communists and Jews they would become discouraged.

UNUSUAL STAMPS

Look through your collection and you will see that most stamps are oblong in shape and fairly standard in size. Some countries print stamps that look a bit different, either because of their shape or size, or because of the materials used. Most countries print these stamps once in a while, but there are a few that print fun stamps most of the time. This is generally because fun stamps are very popular.

CHANGING SHAPE

The most common way of making a set look completely different is to change the shape. The first triangular stamp was produced by the Cape of Good Hope in 1853. At the time, people thought the new shape was outrageous. Today, the triangle is the most popular of the unusual shapes and it is used by many countries, including Ascension (left) and the former Soviet Union (right).

You will find many examples of long, thin stamps such as these commemorative ones from France and The Gambia.

Cut-out shapes have also been used for stamps. This one (below) is from Gibraltar, and the perforations are cut to follow the outline of the peninsula. Sometimes, although the stamp itself is not an unusual shape, the picture is printed on the diagonal, such as this square Colombian stamp (right).

STICKY-BACK STAMPS

Tonga, an archipelago of more than 150 islands in the Pacific Ocean, and Sierra Leone, a country in West Africa, both issue lots of self-adhesive stamps with peel-off backing paper (left and right). The stamps are always cut-out shapes and are highly decorative, so they are very popular with collectors. The U.S. Postal System has also issued a number of sticky-back stamps. If you find one of these, remember that you cannot soak it off. Cut neatly around it or leave the stamp on the envelope.

If you have unused self-adhesive stamps, leave them on their backing paper. Often, this is also very attractive – just look at the back (below) of the Sierra Leone stamp (below right) commemorating human rights.

Occasionally, stamps are issued in unique shapes. The round stamp, the stamp with sloping sides, and the irregular quadrilateral are all from Malaysia. The Christmas commemorative (top) is from Malta.

MATERIAL DIFFERENCES

Almost all stamps are printed on paper. Some of the exceptions are shown here. Plastic 3-D effect stamps with gummed backs have been issued by Bhutan (above right) in a few sets. This stamp shows an Apollo spacecraft leaving its launch rocket. Have you seen the playing record on page 10?

Foil is also used for unusual stamps. Here is a gold foil stamp from Mauritius (below right), an island in the Indian Ocean, showing Prime Minister Sir Seewoosagur Ramgoolam. Some of the cut-out stamps also have foil trimming.

If you find stamps like these on an envelope, it is best not to soak them off as not many of them have ever been used. They are usually bought by collectors.

CINDERELLAS

You may have some stamps in your collection that were issued for local use only. These minor stamps are not included in stamp catalogues and they are not always popular with collectors. Other stamps that do not fit into most collections are non-postage stamps, such as railway stamps, revenue stamps, and telegraph stamps. All these stamps are called cinderellas.

This block of four diamond stamps was issued by a private mail service in Bochum, Germany.

LOCAL MAIL

This local stamp was issued in Shrub Oak, New York.

Local postage stamps are valid only for use within the country or region of issue. They were widely used in the latter part of the nineteenth century, before national postal services were established, in China, Russia, Scandinavia, Germany, and the U.S.A. for delivering local mail within towns.

Some postal services operated outside the areas covered by post offices and issued their own stamps, for example, in the Australian gold fields or high in the Swiss Alps. In very remote areas, such as parts of Colombia and Brazil, local airlines carried mail and issued their own stamps.

STAMPS ON THE RAILWAYS

The world's first public railway, from Stockton to Darlington in England, was opened in 1825. A network of small local railways grew rapidly, and within five years the first mail was carried by train. The railway was often used for urgent letters and packages. Letters were distributed by local delivery but packages were collected from the station.

When mail was sent by train, there was an additional charge. The letter would bear the usual stamp of the Post Office and a railway stamp to show the extra charge (below). Each local railway company had its own stamps.

This stamp was issued by Lundy and Atlantic Coasts Air Lines Ltd.

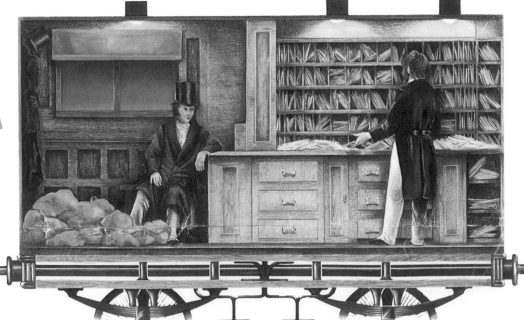

In 1838, mail was first sorted in Traveling Post Offices on board trains. This helped to speed up deliveries.

REVENUE STAMPS

Revenue is the word for money paid to the government, usually as a tax. When tax was paid, the person would receive a receipt with a stamp on it – a revenue stamp like this U.S. Internal Revenue Proprietary stamp and this duty stamp from Western Australia (right, above and below).

Some stamps were printed for use both on mail and on receipts. These have the words "postage and revenue" printed on them, like this example from the Straits Settlements (left).

"TELEGRAM!"

Before most homes had telephones, the quickest way of getting in touch with someone was by sending a telegram. In England, a short message was transmitted by telegraph to the nearest post office, then a local delivery would be made as soon as possible. The telegram sheet had a stamp on it, like this one from the London & District Telegraph Company (right), to show the amount paid.

PRIVATE MAIL

This early German stamp (below left) was issued by a private hand delivery service. In times of strike, enterprising people sometimes set up their own postal service, either for local delivery only, such as the Fresno and San Francisco Bicycle Mail Route (above left) in 1894, or for international distribution by courier, such as this private Toronto–U.S.A. service (above) in 1981.

"MERRY CHRISTMAS!"

Labels are shaped and perforated like stamps, but have no postage value. They are stuck on envelopes for decoration and to carry advertisements or messages. Many old labels, like this one (right) advertising the Art and Industrial Exhibition in 1902, are interesting because they say something about the products and fashions of the time. Modern examples include tourist promotion and Christmas messages.

POSTMARKS

When stamps were first introduced there was great concern that they would be used more than once. If the stamps were soaked off an envelope, then stuck on a new one, they could be used to mail several letters. It was decided to overprint the stamps with a "postmark," to show that they had been used. There were lots of experiments with different inks for postmarks because post offices wanted to use an ink that could not be washed off without ruining the stamp.

If you look at a postmark closely you will see where the letter was sorted and the date it was mailed. If the postmark is made by an automatic machine, the time is sometimes included. Collectors who save postmarks usually stay with one country. The most interesting postmarks are usually found on old letters from the nineteenth century. It is important that the postmark is neat, and clearly shows the place name. It is best to keep the postmark on the envelope.

This cover of 1874 shows a neat duplex cancel.

This is a hand-operated duplex cancel used around 1865.

DUMB CANCELS

The first postmarks were designed to obliterate, or cancel, the stamp just to show that it had been used. These are called dumb cancels. A second postmark was applied to the letter to show where or when the letter was mailed.

CIRCLES, BARS, AND WAVY LINES

As inks improved, postmarks did not have to be so large and ugly, so only the circular section was used. These new-style postmarks are called circular date stamps. Collectors like circular date stamps because they are neat and you can still see the stamp under them.

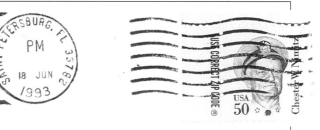

This Australian stamp has been neatly canceled by a circular date stamp.

Japan often uses long bar cancellations.

These U.S. and South African postmarks use wavy lines with a circular date stamp to cancel stamps.

KILLER CANCELS

To avoid having two postmarks, the dumb cancel and details of mailing were combined in a duplex cancel. These are sometimes called killer cancels as they usually make such a mess that the stamps are not worth collecting.

SMALL ADS

A slogan postmark combines a circular date stamp with an advertisement. The first slogan postmarks advertised a national event or promotion.

You will find many modern slogans advertising a local event or promoting a town. Slogan postmarks can spoil stamps, making the stamps useless in a good collection, but the slogans themselves are fascinating to collect.

This German slogan postmark (above) announces the new airmail service to South America.

This postmark (right) features a slogan encouraging Cubans to buy local sugar.

All three of these slogan postmarks (above) from the Netherlands, Gibraltar, and the U.S. encourage people to collect stamps and postmarks.

Slogan postmarks are very popular in France. Here are two typical examples.

REMEMBER, REMEMBER

Commemorative postmarks include the date in the slogan design. They are printed for special events and are often used on decorative envelopes. Modern commemorative postmarks are used for only a few days, whereas early ones were sometimes used up to a year prior to the event.

This German postmark commemorates the 1936 Olympic Games that were held in Berlin.

COVERS

A cover is the name given to a stamped and mailed envelope. Most plain envelopes with stamps are not worth saving. There are two types of covers that are collected, first day covers and commercial covers with interesting postmarks, labels, or other Post Office marks added to them.

FIRST DAY COVERS
A first day cover is a special envelope that has a new set of stamps on it and is mailed on the first day the stamps are available (above left). The envelope is usually illustrated and canceled by hand to give the cover a neat, special postmark. First day covers can be bought a few days before the new stamps are issued.

PRETTY BUT WORTHLESS?
Although they are fun, first day covers are expensive, bulky to collect, and rarely as valuable as unused stamps. However, if there is a new set due that is of special interest to your collection or display, a first day cover makes an attractive addition.

RETURNED TO SENDER
A letter stamped "Returned to Sender" by the post office indicates a particular problem with delivery. "Insufficient address" or "insufficient postage," like this envelope (above), are some of the reasons that might be checked. Other delays might be caused by a poorly wrapped package or a letter stuck in machinery at the sorting office.

DISASTER!
However, sometimes more dramatic events have occurred to damage the mail en route. The postmark on this cover (right) shows that the letter has survived an aircraft fire following a crash.

HOLD UP

A plane hijack (below and right) is an unusual reason for a letter to be late.

UNUSUAL COMMENTS

Any letters with interesting comments from the Post Office are worth saving. If you are lucky enough to have a few good envelopes, it may be worth putting them in an album of their own.

The postmark on this letter (below) reads "Despatched by Tin Can Mail".

MINI MAIL!

This envelope (below) contains a photograph of a letter (bottom of page) from a soldier fighting in the Second World War. In order to save valuable space on transport planes, letters were written on special pages that were photographed. The roll of film was sent to the UK and developed. The letters were then posted on to their destination.

FRAMA LABELS

Frama labels, named after the Swiss company that made the first machine to print them in 1976, are labels with the postage printed on them. They are often used by commercial organizations. The Frama Company now has many competitors.

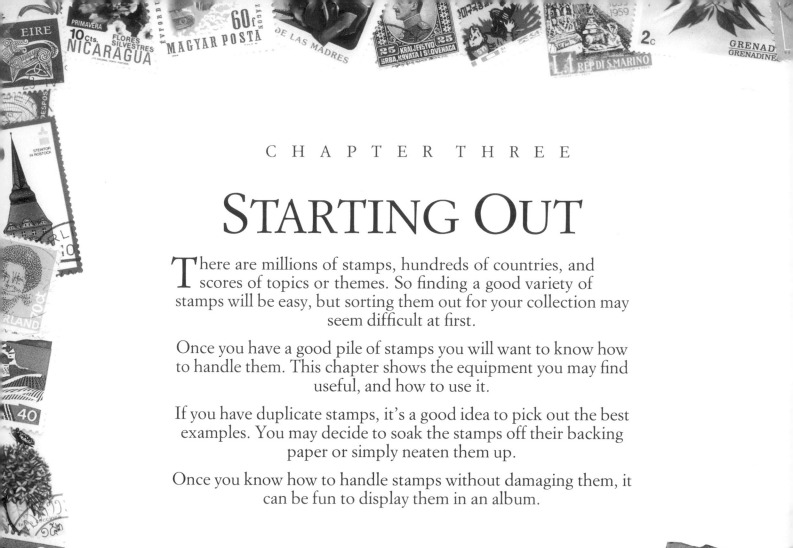

STARTING OUT

There are millions of stamps, hundreds of countries, and scores of topics or themes. So finding a good variety of stamps will be easy, but sorting them out for your collection may seem difficult at first.

Once you have a good pile of stamps you will want to know how to handle them. This chapter shows the equipment you may find useful, and how to use it.

If you have duplicate stamps, it's a good idea to pick out the best examples. You may decide to soak the stamps off their backing paper or simply neaten them up.

Once you know how to handle stamps without damaging them, it can be fun to display them in an album.

HANDLE WITH CARE!

Stamps are small, fragile pieces of paper, so it is important to be careful when handling them. Here is some simple equipment that will help you identify and care for your stamps.

WATERMARK DETECTOR
Watermarks (top right) are found on most old stamps. They were used to make forgeries more difficult (see pages 19 and 32–33). Sometimes watermarks can be seen very easily when you hold the stamp up to a light or lay it face down on a dark surface. Sometimes you need to use a watermark detector.

- The detector (above) looks like a thin plastic wallet. Inside, it has a small, firm plastic pad on which to place the stamp face down and a small sealed sachet of ink.
- When the detector is closed, the sachet of ink lies on top of the stamp. Squeeze the wallet and the shape of the watermark will show through the ink.

PERFORATION GAUGE
This is used to measure the number of perforations on every 2 cm of stamp edge. There are two types of gauge.

- One is made of cardboard or plastic with rows of dots that show how many perforation holes fit into 2 cm. Place the stamp on top of the gauge. Fit it on the different rows of dots until you find the one which shows a dot in each perforation. The number beside the row of dots tells you the size of the perforations.
- The second gauge looks like a clear plastic ruler. Place the stamp flat on a piece of paper and lay the gauge on top. When the perforations on the stamp match the lines on the gauge, read the number alongside.

The perforation gauge shows that this Chinese stamp is perf 15, or 15 holes per 2 cm.

MAGNIFYING GLASS
It can be fun to spot more detail on an intricate design. A small, high-magnification glass is useful when you take stamp collecting more seriously and begin to study tiny details on stamps.

$60 $150 $7.50 $24

Even a small difference in color can affect the value of a stamp. The dull orange version of this Australian fourpence stamp is worth about $60. The lemon version is worth $150.

On this 40-cent stamp from Singapore, the perforations make the difference. The stamp with larger perforations is worth approximately $7.50 while the other is worth $24.

TWEEZERS

Even clean hands can damage your stamps because your skin is slightly acidic; prolonged contact may cause the paper to deteriorate. Also, the tiny perforations around the edge of the stamp bend easily. Use tweezers to avoid this.

- Buy metal tweezers that have smooth, rounded ends. Sharp tweezers with rough edges or points can puncture stamps.
- Hold the tweezers firmly on the textured gripper area with your thumb halfway down the top and your finger underneath.
- Pinch the tweezers together gently to close the ends. Practice on a piece of paper, then try picking up stamps. You will soon find that you can sort stamps much more quickly with tweezers!

COLOR GUIDE

A color guide is made up of a number of cards of different color shades, attached at one end so that they open out like a fan. Lay the color guide over or near the stamp, matching the different colors until you find the right one.

This is useful for checking the exact color of a stamp with a plain design. Older stamps, in use for several years, were often printed in many shades of basically the same color.

THE GOOD, THE BAD, AND THE UGLY

These pages are all about having a good collection. At first, every collector saves all the stamps he or she can find. When the collection grows, the damaged stamps begin to look ugly and they have to be sorted out.

Here are three examples of the same Ceylonese stamp with progressively better postmarks.

BUILDING A GOOD COLLECTION
- Pick out all stamps that are the same. Sort out the best stamp to keep. Put the others into a swap book.
- Do not buy damaged stamps or take them in exchange for your swaps.
- Pinpoint important stamps in poor condition from your collection. Keep them in place but look for better examples to replace them.

GOOD STAMPS
Good stamps are not torn or creased. They are not broken around the edge or badly marked in any way. The postmarks on them are small and neat. They are the ideal stamps to have in your collection.

These are the ideal stamps to collect. Not all the stamps in your collection will be this good (left).

BAD STAMPS
Bad stamps are creased, broken, damaged around the edge, or torn. They may be rubbed thin from use or during soaking off. The perforations may have been broken. There are always bad stamps in a new album – picking them out and swapping them or replacing them is all part of the fun of collecting.

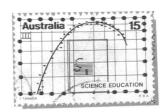

Look out for better examples to replace damaged stamps in your collection (left and above).

UGLY STAMPS

Ugly stamps are not broken or torn but they have heavy or ugly postmarks on them. Big, black, smudged markings, and dirt and stains are sometimes found on stamps and covers and these make the collection look messy. Pick these out and get rid of them as soon as possible.

SOCKED ON THE NOSE

Some collectors like to have a circular postmark right in the middle of the stamp (below). The postmark must clearly show all the details. The date, name of the town, and other information are all extremely neat and easy to read. This type of postmark is called "socked on the nose." There are not many postmarks like this, and part of the fun of collecting them is finding the occasional example.

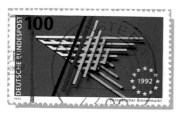

These stamps (above) have ugly postmarks so that you cannot see the design clearly. The stamps on the left are neatly "socked on the nose."

GOOD AND BAD PERFORATIONS

These stamps show the difference between good and bad perforations. The Pakistani stamp on the right has neat perforations all the way around it. The stamp from North Borneo (below left) has uneven perforations, especially along the top edge; the stamp from New Zealand (below right) has a broken corner.

Sometimes the perforations are only a little uneven (far left), but watch out for stamps with ugly missing corners (left).

FIRST THINGS FIRST

To prepare stamps for your album, you will have to soak them off their backing paper, dry them, and press them ready for mounting in your album. Soaking stamps can be fun, but it can be messy too. Before you begin soaking stamps, make sure you have a clear place to put a bowl of water where it will not be in the way.

SOAKING OFF STAMPS

Fill a bowl with *cold* water about 3 inches (7.5 cm) deep, and put it on a tray (**1**) with a clean, dry dish towel. Cut carefully around the stamp and postmark (**2**). (Keep any stamps on brightly colored paper separate (**3**) as this may stain the rest of your stamps and put them in *hot* water with a little dishwashing liquid. Remove them after a few seconds when the stamps float off.) Push a few stamps under the water (**4**), and allow them to soak. Time 10 to 15 minutes, then check that the stamps are beginning to float off their backing paper (**5**). Most stamps will come off their backing paper easily. If not, leave them for another 5 minutes. Place each stamp face down on your hand and gently bend the paper back (**6**) until it peels away. Finally, lay each stamp picture-down on the dish towel to dry (**7**).

FLOATING OFF STAMPS

Some people prefer floating stamps off as this method does not wet the surface of the stamps. Soaking stamps does remove a little of the surface coating but this is only important if you have very special or valuable stamps in your collection. Floating off stamps takes a lot longer; the stamps will curl more as they dry; and they are more difficult to flatten.

Fill a bowl with *cold* water about 3 inches (7.5 cm) deep. Lay your stamps carefully on the water surface so they float.

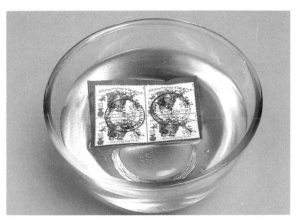

Leave the stamps floating for 20 to 30 minutes. The stamp stays dry, but the paper underneath soaks up water and dampens the glue.

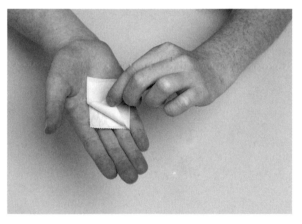

Lift the stamps out of the water one at a time. Place a stamp picture-side-down on your hand and carefully peel off the backing paper.

Place the stamps picture-side-down on a clean, dry dish towel or a piece of thick paper towel to dry. (The glue will be sticky until the stamps have dried.)

DRYING AND FLATTENING STAMPS

Stamps take a few hours to dry completely. Do not try to speed up the drying as this may damage the stamps and will definitely make them curl more.

To flatten the dry stamps, lay them carefully between two clean pieces of paper. Place a heavy book on top and leave them overnight. You should press your stamps for a couple of days. Putting the stamps in their album or stockbook helps.

SELF-ADHESIVE STAMPS

The gum that is used on some older self-adhesive stamps does not soften on soaking or floating. Instead of removing them from the paper, cut out a neat border of envelope around them.

To flatten the dried stamps, lay them carefully between two pieces of clean paper. Put a heavy book on top and leave them overnight.

WHICH ALBUM?

Once your collection starts to grow, you will need an album to keep your stamps safe and to display them attractively. There are a lot of different albums to choose from. Here are some of the more common types.

FIRST ALBUMS

A printed album, with pages marked in squares, will start you off on the right track (left). Because all the pages are well organized, you can start putting in your stamps right away. The traditional album is arranged by country, but you can also buy albums to arrange your stamps by subject, such as birds or flowers.

These albums are inexpensive and are very good if you have stamps from many different countries. However, if you have a large number of stamps from one country, buy a simple album that can have extra pages added, or put them in a separate album.

ADVANCED ALBUMS

These are larger, more expensive, and more flexible (below). Some are for collecting one country and are printed with pictures of the stamps in the right order. Others have light grids to help you mount your stamps neatly. These albums are for collectors who want to mount their stamps in their own way, with notes.

SPRINGBACK ALBUMS
The leaves of this traditional album are held by a spring in the spine. They are removed by folding back the cover against the spring. These popular albums hold the leaves together well but do not lie flat when opened.

RING-BINDER ALBUMS
These albums have their pages held in place by between two and twenty rings that clip together. They are very useful, because they lie perfectly flat when open. However, try to avoid albums with only two rings, as the pages can easily tear.

PEG-FITTING ALBUMS
The pages of these albums are held in place by two or four pegs that clip into the spine and will almost lie flat when open. Sometimes the mechanism to lock the pegs in place can be difficult to use.

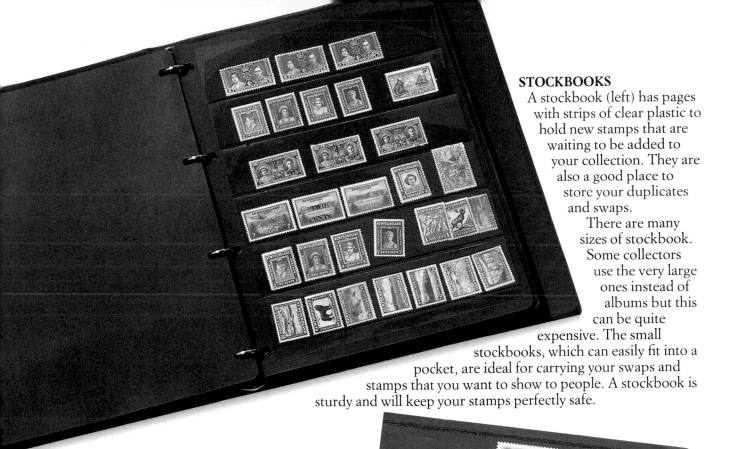

STOCKBOOKS

A stockbook (left) has pages with strips of clear plastic to hold new stamps that are waiting to be added to your collection. They are also a good place to store your duplicates and swaps.

There are many sizes of stockbook. Some collectors use the very large ones instead of albums but this can be quite expensive. The small stockbooks, which can easily fit into a pocket, are ideal for carrying your swaps and stamps that you want to show to people. A stockbook is sturdy and will keep your stamps perfectly safe.

STOCKCARDS

Stockcards with two or three plastic strips and a clear plastic cover are also available (right). Professional stamp collectors use these to display stamps. However, they do not withstand much wear and tear so they are not recommended for your swaps.

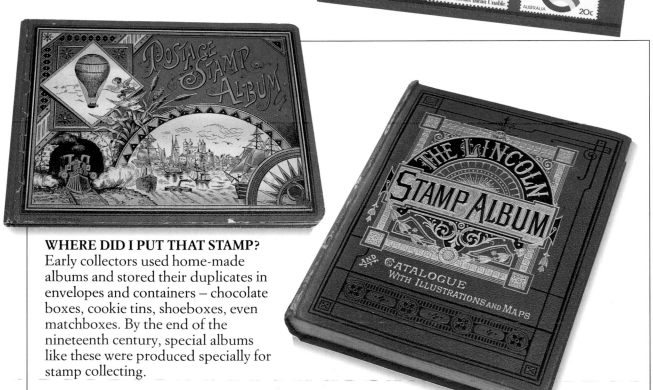

WHERE DID I PUT THAT STAMP?

Early collectors used home-made albums and stored their duplicates in envelopes and containers – chocolate boxes, cookie tins, shoeboxes, even matchboxes. By the end of the nineteenth century, special albums like these were produced specially for stamp collecting.

51

ARRANGING YOUR ALBUM

Definitive Issue
65

ORCHID

ARCHER FISH

SINGAPORE

BUTTERFLY FISH

HARLEQUIN

TWO-SPOTTED GOURAMI

SINGAPORE

BLACK-NAPED TERN

ORCHID

ORCHID

SINGAPORE

WHITE-RUMPED SHAMA

WHITE-THROATED KINGFISHER

WHITE-BELLIED SEA EAGLE

WATERMARK
MULTIPLE St. EDWARD'S CROWN CA

PRINTERS
HARRISON + SONS
DE LA RUE

The best collections are carefully arranged with notes about the stamps. Arranging stamps is an aspect of stamp collecting that most collectors enjoy and take pride in. Clever displays of stamps can look very impressive, and there are lots of ways to mount stamps in groups. Here are some tips:

- Take time to make a balanced pattern of the stamps.

- A square is the simplest arrangement if all the stamps are the same size.

- The top and bottom rows may be shorter if the number of stamps in the set do not make a neat square shape.

- Some sets have stamps of different sizes, but try to keep the stamps in order from the lowest to the highest value.

NOTE WELL
Write the title, date of issue, and name of the printer beside the stamp. Notes on the design can also be added. Most of this information can be found in a stamp catalogue.

If you are using a pen, keep the lettering simple. Before deciding on your style take time to practice. Try capitals and small letters to see which you prefer. It will not take long to write your notes neatly and attractively once you have decided how to go about it.

Self-adhesive titles and labels (above right) make your album pages look neat. They come complete with instructions. You can also create titles using letters that can be rubbed onto the page using a tool called a burnisher (right).

MOUNTING STAMPS

Take time to make sure that your stamps are fixed to the pages neatly. It is usual to keep stamps of the same size together and to arrange the older stamps on the page before the more modern stamps. Generally, it's a good idea not to mix unused and used stamps – keep them separate on the page or on different pages in the album.

It is best to use stamp hinges (left) in your first album. They are cheap and simple to use, and easy to remove when you want to change a stamp's position.

HOW TO USE STAMP HINGES

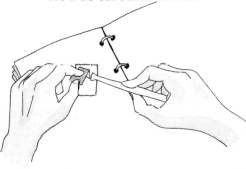

1 Lightly lick the smaller folded part of the hinge.

2 Press the hinge on the back of the stamp. It should be as near to the top edge of the stamp as possible. Be careful that the hinge does not show behind the perforations.

3 Now lick the remaining part of the hinge.

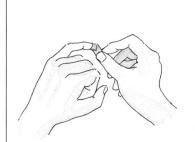

4 Carefully put the stamp in place on the page. Use tweezers with smooth rounded ends to position hinges and stamps. The glue takes a little while to harden so you can adjust the stamp slightly to make sure that it is straight. If you want to move the stamp, do not try and remove it right away. The glue will peel off easily only when it is completely dry.

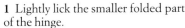

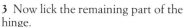

PLASTIC MOUNTS

These are clear plastic strips, with an opening to put the stamp in, that are gummed on the back. Plastic mounts (right) are expensive and can be bought in strips or cut for individual stamps. You need a special cutter to make neat strips.

Plastic mounts are best for specialized collections where there are only a few stamps on each page. These mounts are difficult to remove so use them only if you know you are not going to change the page. Stick the mount to the page before putting in the stamp.

BUILDING UP YOUR COLLECTION

To build up your collection, the first thing to do is to tell everyone you know that you are collecting stamps – family, friends, and neighbors. Ask them to save all their stamps. Sometimes the postmarks or the whole envelopes look good in a collection, so ask for the stamps to be left on their envelopes.

STAMP PACKETS

Stamp packets, which hold from five to twenty stamps, are available. The packets may specialize in countries but, more often, they contain stamps that share the same theme. Larger packets, holding up to a thousand different stamps, are better value for the money. They will give you plenty of material to sort out since they hold stamps of all types from all over the world.

These packets (left) are typical – one contains stamps from western Europe, one has stamps featuring flowers, and one contains a mixture of pictorial stamps.

BAGS OF STAMPS

Enormous bags of stamps that are still on paper are often sold by weight in stamp shops or offered in magazines. These are called kiloware (right). They may contain stamps of just one country or a mixture of stamps from all over the world. Sometimes, if you are lucky, there are better stamps in a kiloware pack than in the small packets, but you will find lots of duplicates!

NEW STAMPS

Look for advertisements announcing new stamps. You may have to act promptly as small post offices often run out very quickly. Some large post offices have philatelic services offering new issues for longer periods than ordinary post offices.

YEAR PACKS

Post offices in some countries have year packs that contain the commemorative issues from the previous year, together with notes.

IN THE MAIL

Look in the back of any philatelic magazine and you will find lots of mail-order companies to choose from. Mail-order services are useful but the postage can be expensive.

STAMP SHOPS

Stamp shops have all but disappeared in the United States, but still exist in other countries. These shops often sell inexpensive bags of stamps, like kiloware, or have special offers on packets.

STAMP SHOWS

Stamp shows (above and right) are well worth a visit. Stamp dealers' stands offer all sorts of stamps, from bags of stamps (kiloware) and packets to individual stamps and covers, catalogues, albums, and equipment. Look for pages of stamps from old albums that are sold as single items – they are often good buys.

EXHIBITIONS

Exhibitions display collections and competition entries. Looking at the displays (left) will give you plenty of ideas for your collection. There are always stands where you can buy stamps and equipment, and friendly people to help young collectors, especially if you go when it is not too busy. Look in your library or local paper for details.

GOING, GOING, GONE

At an auction, stamps are sold in lots that may contain only one or two expensive items or a real jumble of stamps, albums, and stockbooks. A catalogue is available before the auction, and lists all the lots. It can be exciting to visit an auction to see valuable stamps sold for lots of money, even if you are not going to buy anything yourself.

USING A CATALOGUE

All postage stamps are listed in stamp catalogues. Some catalogues list stamps from all over the world; others will tell you about the stamps from just one country. There are also catalogues of thematic stamps.

A catalogue gives two prices for each stamp, one for a new stamp and another for a used stamp. These prices are known as the catalogue value. It is fun to look up your best stamps to find out how much they are worth.

Most catalogues are expensive, so if you cannot afford to buy one, take a look in the library. The U.S. Postal Service sells a pocket-size color catalogue which pictures every U.S. stamp ever issued.

Catalogues tell you what stamps a country has issued, when, and why. They also give details of perforation size, watermarks, design, and printer, as well as a guide to how much the stamps are worth.

IMPERFECT PRICE
This Hong Kong 1873 four-cent stamp (left) has only 12½ perforations per 2 cm instead of 14. In the 1933 Stanley Gibbons catalogue (right), this error was listed as £16 ($24). Today, it is worth £3,500 (over $5,000).

PERFECT PRICE
The value given in the catalogue is the price for which the dealer will sell the stamp when it is in perfect condition. If you are buying stamps, you will probably pay less than the catalogue value. The price depends on the condition of the stamp. Any defects, even small ones, will greatly reduce the value of a stamp.

So don't expect to sell the stamps in your collection for that price!

- The date when the stamp was issued
- The stamps issued
- A guide to the value of the stamp
- The reason why the stamps were issued

FIND THAT STAMP!

Follow these simple steps to find one of your stamps in a catalogue.

1 What country does the stamp come from?

2 Look for the year of issue on the stamp. If there isn't a date on the stamp, look for one on the postmark. Sometimes the picture on the stamp will give a clue to the year when the stamp was printed.

3 Look at the designs of stamps in the catalogue. If there isn't a picture of your stamp, there will be a description. Sometimes there will be a picture of another stamp from the same series that looks very similar.

4 Once you find the set in the catalogue, look for the stamps with the same face value as your stamp.

5 Check that all the details in the catalogue are the same as your stamp. Then read the other information – you may want to write notes from the catalogue in your album.

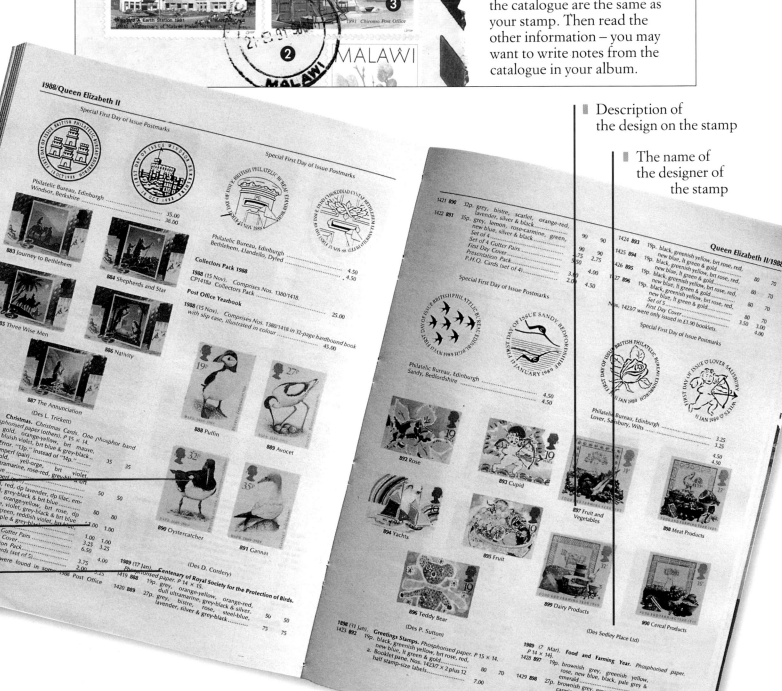

COLLECTING BY COUNTRY

M ost collectors begin by collecting the stamps of the world. This is a good way to start, but you will probably find that there are far too many stamps to continue. Before long, you will have to decide whether you want to specialize in the stamps of one country or one continent.

Stamps can tell you a lot about the history, geography, politics, and industry of a country. Commemorative stamps will feature historic events and important citizens; special stamps will show something of the life of the country.

You may decide to collect the stamps of your own country. It will be easy for you to buy new issues from the Post Office and to swap stamps missing from your collection with a fellow collector. Or you may have a friend or relative who lives overseas who will send you stamps. That way you can learn more about another country.

The next pages show you a selection of stamps from the countries of five continents.

OCEANIA

AFRICA

You can trace the history of Africa through your stamps. The Dark Continent, as Africa was known in the nineteenth century, was largely unknown until European explorers discovered its magnificent lakes and waterfalls, soaring mountains, mighty rivers, and thick jungles full of wildlife.

GAMBIA
This striking 1965 stamp celebrates the Gambia's independence.

NAMIBIA
The 1976 cover (below) was issued when Namibia was known as South West Africa. Above, you can see a stamp with the new name, Namibia.

ZIMBABWE
Victoria Falls (above) are one of the world's most spectacular waterfalls. This 1955 Rhodesia and Nyasaland stamp (above right) shows the falls and David Livingstone, who discovered them and named them in 1855.

The walled city of Great Zimbabwe is one of the greatest African mysteries. The massive stone ruins were built from granite blocks from the eleventh century to the fourteenth century but nobody knows why. The modern state of Zimbabwe is named after this ancient center for religion and the gold trade. This 1985 stamp (below) features some of the ruins of Great Zimbabwe.

LESOTHO
This 1967 stamp (above) commemorates the first anniversary of independence.

NIGERIA
The people of Benin, once part of Nigeria, were famous for their sculptures of human heads. This stamp (right) features a Benin mask. The stamp (below) shows Nigerian warriors.

CHAD
This stamp (above) shows a man working hard at the traditional craft of tanning leather.

GHANA
This stamp (below), issued when Ghana was known as the Gold Coast, shows the cocoa pods, which grow in Ghana.

MOROCCO
These two Moroccan stamps (above) show a man and woman in colorful traditional costumes.

EGYPT
One of the earliest civilizations (above), ancient Egypt existed in Africa five thousand years ago. This Egyptian stamp (right) shows the front entrance of the temple of Ramses II at Abu Simbel.

KENYA
This stamp (above) commemorates the independence of the Republic of Kenya in 1964.

TANZANIA
The stamp (top) is a commemorative issue, marking the 10th anniversary of the union of postal services all over Africa. The tsetse fly (above) is a common pest all over Africa, and spreads disease among cattle and humans.

UGANDA AND RWANDA
Some of the world's largest mammals live in the wide grassy plains and lush mountain forests of Africa. This Ugandan stamp (above) of 1977 shows elephants and commemorates the 25th Safari Rally in 1977.

This stamp from Rwanda (right) shows a rare mountain gorilla.

SOUTH AFRICA
RSA on this stamp (right) stands for the Republic of South Africa. This stamp features a colorful cactus.

61

THE AMERICAS

People in Europe first began to know about the Americas after Christopher Columbus sailed there in 1492. Other explorers from Spain and Portugal, France, Holland, and England soon followed. They found a vast and exciting "New World" with huge rivers, tremendously high mountains, and enormous stretches of forest and jungle. The New World also contained a different people: Native Americans who had crossed from Asia when the two continents were joined.

Today, the Americas contain many different countries. Their stamps provide a pictorial record of their continent.

CANADA
This set of stamps (above) illustrates the growth of the federation of Canada, between 1867 and 1949.

Canada issued one of the first commemorative stamps in 1898 (above). It commemorates the Commonwealth of Nations and has "Xmas 1898" printed across the bottom.

UNITED STATES OF AMERICA

In the pioneer days of the late nineteenth century, mail was very important to those people who were venturing into new territory. The Pony Express was established on April 3, 1860 to link the eastern states with California. Previously, the journey from St. Joseph, Missouri, to Sacramento and San Francisco took three weeks. The Pony Express used 190 relay stations with 500 horses and 80 first-class riders to reduce the scheduled time to ten days (right).

One of the most famous riders, Buffalo Bill Cody, once rode 384 miles (618 kilometers) nonstop except to change horses. The all-time record was achieved in November 1860 to bring President Abraham Lincoln's inaugural address 2,000 miles (3,200 kilometers) from the east coast to the west in just 7 days, 17 hours. The completion of the telegraph service to San Francisco in 1861 heralded the end of the Pony Express.

COLOMBIA
This 1985 stamp (above) shows the ocelot, which lives in the forests and arid brushlands of Colombia.

The Declaration of Independence was adopted on July 4, 1776 at the beginning of the American War of Independence (1775– 1783). This sheet (left) containing the flags of all 50 U.S. states was issued at the time of the Bicentennial celebrations in 1976.

Canada
Canada 17
Canada in 1905
Le Canada en 1905

Canada 17
Canada since 1949
Le Canada depuis 1949

GREENLAND

CANADA

UNITED STATES OF AMERICA

BAHAMAS

CUBA
HAITI — DOMINICAN REPUBLIC
BELIZE
GUATEMALA — HONDURAS
NICARAGUA
PANAMA

VENEZUELA — GUYANA
COLOMBIA — SURINAM
ECUADOR — FRENCH GUIANA

BRAZIL

PERU

BOLIVIA

PARAGUAY

URUGUAY

CHILE — ARGENTINA

NICARAGUA
Two competing companies petitioned Congress for money to build a canal through Central America. The company with the rights in Panama used this stamp, picturing an active volcano, to convince Congress to give them the grant, rather than the company with the rights in Nicaragua.

BELIZE
In 1962, a disastrous hurricane swept through Belize, known then as British Honduras. This stamp (left) was overprinted to raise funds for relief work.

FALKLAND ISLANDS
This cover (below) was canceled by hand during the Argentinian invasion of the Falklands Islands in 1982 because the Argentinians did not want to use the Falklands Islands postmark. Later, Argentina added its own postmark for the Islas Malvinas, as the Falklands Islands are known in Argentina.

CUBA
This 1982 stamp (above) features coffee, one of Cuba's major exports.

ARGENTINA
The largest of all penguins, the emperor penguin featured on this stamp (above), lives in the southern part of Argentina.

ASIA

Asia is the world's largest continent. It contains the highest place on earth, Mount Everest (29,000 feet, 8,848 meters) in Nepal, and the lowest place on earth, the Dead Sea (1,300 feet, 395 meters below sea level) in Israel.

The continent comprises five main regions: the Middle East, the Central Asian Republics, East Asia, the Indian sub-continent, and Southeast Asia. Some of the world's great civilizations, and the five main religions – Buddhism, Christianity, Hinduism, Islam, and Judaism – began in Asia.

Because of its dramatic history, Asia is a good place to look for stamps showing the world's most ancient art, buildings, cities, and costumes.

IRAQ
This Iraqi stamp (above) features an Assyrian sculpture. The Assyrian Empire dominated Mesopotamia, the former name of Iraq, between the ninth and seventh centuries BC.

IRAN
From 1941 to 1979, Iran was ruled by Shah Mohammed Reza, shown on the stamp above.

CHINA
One of the world's first great civilizations existed along the Yellow River in China four thousand years ago. Around 200 BC, the Great Wall of China was built. It extends 2,000 miles (3,220 kilometers). The Great Wall of China is featured on this 1992 stamp (above).

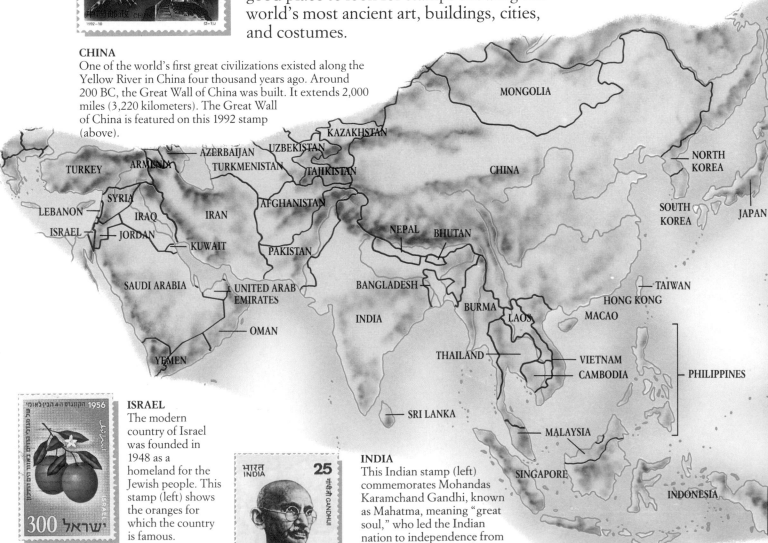

ISRAEL
The modern country of Israel was founded in 1948 as a homeland for the Jewish people. This stamp (left) shows the oranges for which the country is famous.

INDIA
This Indian stamp (left) commemorates Mohandas Karamchand Gandhi, known as Mahatma, meaning "great soul," who led the Indian nation to independence from the British Empire in 1947.

VIETNAM

This stamp was issued in 1955. It pictures boat people fleeing to the south from North Vietnam after the Communists took it over from the French in 1954.

JAPAN

This beautiful 1969 stamp (left) shows a traditional Japanese painting.

The national flag of Japan is dramatically displayed on the stamp (above).

THE PHILIPPINES

Two of the Philippines' most famous citizens, Ferdinand and Imelda Marcos, the former President and his wife, are illustrated on this 1965 stamp (below).

SINGAPORE

Singapore is an island with a fine natural harbor. This stamp (above) illustrates the modern city's mass rapid transportation system.

Singapore is known as the Lion City (*singa pura* means lion city). Here the lion is featured on a set of stamps issued in 1959 (right).

THAILAND

This 1982 stamp (left) shows King Rama III of Thailand in traditional Thai costume.

MALAYSIA

Malaysia is one of the world's largest producers of rubber. This 1968 stamp (above) shows the latex being collected from a groove cut into a rubber tree, and a set of tires, one of the major uses of rubber.

BANGLADESH

Bangladesh is a tiny country bordering India. This stamp shows mail being delivered.

SRI LANKA

Tea production is a major industry in Sri Lanka, formerly known as Ceylon. This stamp (right) shows a Sri Lankan woman plucking tea leaves.

HONG KONG

These stamps (above) were issued in 1891 to commemorate the 50th anniversary of the colony. They are some of the first commemorative stamps ever issued. Only 50,000 copies were issued, and a report at the time said that in the rush to buy the new stamps "two Portuguese were crushed to death, and a Dutch sailor was beaten to death."

EUROPE

Although Europe is the smallest continent, it is made up of almost 50 countries, and its people speak over 50 different languages. These people, their languages, and their culture, together with the contrasts of geography and climate make Europe a continent full of variety. This variety is reflected in the many different stamps you can collect.

EIRE
Eire is the Gaelic name for the Republic of Ireland.

SWITZERLAND
This Swiss stamp (above) commemorates the 1954 football World Cup.

NETHERLANDS
This 1962 Dutch stamp (below) features the canals and windmills of the Netherlands.

ICELAND
Fishing is one of the main industries of Iceland and is featured on many stamps (above).

FRANCE
France is well known for its fine wine and food and its fabulous fashions.

This 1975 stamp (right) displays the four most important industries of France: cereals, wine, meat, and steel.

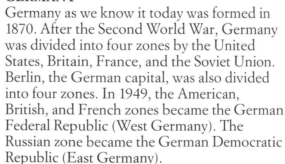

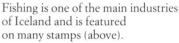

PORTUGAL
This 1953 stamp from Portugal (above) commemorates the fiftieth anniversary of the Automobile Club.

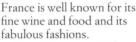
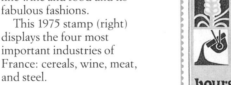

GREAT BRITAIN
The Greenwich Meridian, shown on this 1984 stamp (above), is another name for 0° longitude. It is the point from which all other countries of the world take the time.

BELGIUM
This Belgian stamp (above) features a small, old-fashioned train.

GERMANY
Germany as we know it today was formed in 1870. After the Second World War, Germany was divided into four zones by the United States, Britain, France, and the Soviet Union. Berlin, the German capital, was also divided into four zones. In 1949, the American, British, and French zones became the German Federal Republic (West Germany). The Russian zone became the German Democratic Republic (East Germany).

Berlin was divided in 1961 when East Germany built an enormous wall reinforcing the border. West Berlin was cut off from the rest of West Germany, so it issued its own stamps. In December 1989, the Berlin Wall was demolished (right) and on October 3, 1990, Germany was reunited. This stamp (above) was issued to commemorate the reunification.

SWEDEN
This 1960 Swedish stamp (left) is a commemorative. It is imperforate at the top and bottom, so probably came from a machine.

FINLAND
Suomi is the Finnish name for Finland. This 1947 stamp (right) shows a mail bus traveling alongside one of the country's many lakes.

DENMARK
Denmark is part of Scandinavia that sticks up into the Baltic from the mainland of Europe. This stamp features an old castle (right).

ICELAND

FAROE ISLANDS

THE FAROE ISLANDS
Faroe Islands means "sheep islands." They are found between the Shetland Islands (off Scotland) and Iceland. This stamp commemorates the International Year of the Child in 1979 and illustrates one of the islands' main industries.

SPAIN
This dramatic stamp (below) of 1965 illustrates Spain's controversial national sport, bullfighting.

ITALY
This Italian stamp depicting the Castello di Mussomeli (right) is one of a large set of current definitive stamps.

GREECE
Greece is the home of democracy and the Olympic Games. This stamp (right) illustrates the Parthenon, one of the finest buildings of ancient Greece.

OCEANIA

Oceania is the name given to the islands of the central and south Pacific Ocean, including the continent of Australia.

NAURU
Fishing is obviously important to the islanders of Nauru. These two stamps depict the same theme but in different styles.

This miniature sheet of 1990 (above) features the first stamps of the six states – New South Wales, Queensland, South Australia, Tasmania, Victoria, and Western Australia.

AUSTRALIA
Australia is a large island between the Indian and Pacific oceans, comprising six states and two territories. There are many plants and animals unique to Australia. The best known is the kangaroo. When the states joined together and formed the Commonwealth of Australia, the first stamp showed a kangaroo in front of a map of the country (below right).

NORFOLK ISLAND
Norfolk Island, a territory of Australia located in the Pacific Ocean, was discovered by Captain James Cook in 1774. It issues its own stamps, even though it is so tiny.

PAPUA NEW GUINEA

AUSTRALIA

TASMANIA
The island of Tasmania, off the southern coast of Australia, is one of the continent's states.

PACIFIC ISLANDS

The islands of the Pacific Ocean are divided into three groups: Micronesia (the little islands), which describes the tiny atolls of the west Pacific; Melanesia (the black islands), which includes the islands northeast of Australia from New Guinea to New Caledonia; and Polynesia (the many islands), the volcanic islands and coral atolls of the central Pacific.

PAPUA NEW GUINEA

Much of Papua New Guinea is covered by tropical rain forest where many exotic species live, including the frog pictured on this stamp (above).

PITCAIRN ISLANDS

This Pitcairn Islands stamp (left) features Fletcher Christian aboard the *Bounty*. Christian led a mutiny against the ship's captain, William Bligh, in 1789. The mutineers eventually established a community on the Pitcairn Islands, in the eastern Pacific Ocean.

SAMOA

Louis Antoine de Bougainville, a French naval officer, explored the Pacific between 1766 and 1769 and visited Samoa. This stamp (right) commemorates the bicentenary of his visit and features the beautiful shrub, bougainvillea, that was named after him.

FIJI

As with many islands of the south Pacific, Fiji is a member of the British Commonwealth. The stamp (left) commemorates Commonwealth Day 1963. The stamp below shows a typical sailing boat used in the Fiji islands.

NEW ZEALAND

Early postal systems in New Zealand were very haphazard, dependent on any ship that happened to be passing or visiting the islands. It could take two years for a letter to Europe to receive a reply! The post offices inland were very primitive, sometimes as simple as a plank of wood resting on two bales of wool to make a counter for the postmaster during his hours of business. The stamps below feature sheep, New Zealand's major industry.

This stamp illustrates one of the shyest, rarest birds in the world, the kiwi of New Zealand.

Map labels:
NAURU
SOLOMON ISLANDS
KIRIBATI
TUVALU
VANUATU
WESTERN SAMOA
FIJI
TONGA
NORFOLK ISLAND
NEW ZEALAND

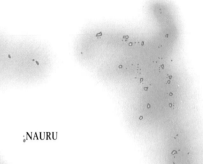

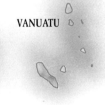

KEEPING UP WITH CHANGE

Collecting stamps by country can sometimes be quite a challenge. War, new-found independence, and other political and social changes mean that countries' borders and names often alter.

These engravings (above) of early stamps from Tanganyika and Zanzibar are taken from a 1933 Stanley Gibbons catalogue. The Tanzanian stamp of 1990 (left) commemorates International Literacy Year.

SPOT THE SIMILARITY!

Sometimes, a country's new name is not very different from the old one. When Tanganyika and Zanzibar merged in 1964, the new country was known as Tanzania. At other times, it can be hard to spot the similarity! For example, when Ceylon became independent in 1972, its name changed to Sri Lanka.

Mount Kilimanjaro (left) is one of the most dramatic sights in Tanzania.

FOURTEEN NEW COUNTRIES, FOURTEEN NEW STAMPS

The breakup of the former Soviet Union into independent nations in 1992 led to the issue of a number of new stamps. Some were Soviet stamps with overprints, such as these for Latvia (**1**) and the Ukraine (**2**). Others were new designs, such as these for Russia (**3**), Lithuania (**4**), Belarus (**5**), Turkmenistan (**6**), and Uzbekistan (**7**).

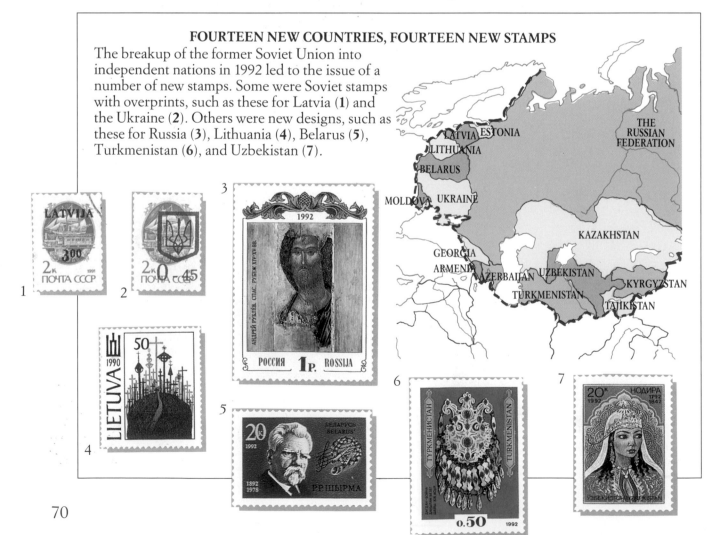

NAME CHANGES

Some countries have changed their identities more than once. These two sets of stamps show two name changes for one country. In 1924, Rhodesia divided into Northern and Southern Rhodesia. Between 1954 and 1964, the two countries merged to form the Central African Federation.

Southern Rhodesia was renamed Rhodesia in October 1964 and the first stamps (below left) appeared in May 1965. The country was renamed yet again – as Zimbabwe – on independence in April 1980 (below right).

OLD FOR NEW

When a country changes its name, stamps are among the first items to show the new name. When a country does not change its name, existing stamps may be overprinted "Independence," like this one from Jamaica (right), until new stamps are ready.

CZECHO-SLOVAKIA!

Once part of the vast Austro-Hungarian empire, Czechoslovakia became an independent country in 1918. It was formed from the Czech-inhabited regions of Bohemia, Moravia, and Silesia, and the Slovak-inhabited part of Hungary known as Slovakia.

Czechoslovakia became a communist country in 1948 and remained united until 1992, when the Velvet Revolution (so called because the change of power was peaceful) led to an end to communism and Czechoslovakia divided into two separate nations: the Czech Republic and the Slovak Republic.

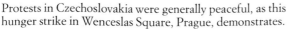
Protests in Czechoslovakia were generally peaceful, as this hunger strike in Wenceslas Square, Prague, demonstrates.

COLLECTING BY THEME

Instead of saving stamps from a particular country or continent, some philatelists collect stamps which all show the same subject. This is called thematic or topical collecting. Collecting by theme can be as simple or complicated as you like. For example, you might want to collect as many stamps as you can that feature cars, or try and build up a collection showing the historical development of the motor car.

Remember that you do not have to limit your thematic collection to stamps alone. You can include covers, postcards, special postmarks, or even extracts from magazines as features in your album. However, all the extras should highlight the importance of the stamps.

TOP TEN THEMES

1 BIRDS

2 SPACE

3 TRAINS

4 CATS

5 SHIPS

6 ANIMALS

7 AVIATION

8 FLOWERS

9 BUTTERFLIES

10 MEDICINE

The space race in the 1960s created enormous interest around the world, and many countries feature space-related subjects on their stamps. These stamps are interesting to collect, as you can trace the history of space travel with each new issue.

APOLLO SOYUZ SPACE TEST PROJECT
UNITED STATES · 1975
10c
US 10c
APOLLO SOYUZ 1975

3c
DOMINICA
VIKING MISSION TO MARS

RF
POSTES 0.50
11-12 JUILLET 1962
PREMIERE LIAISON DE TELEVISION PAR SATELLITE
TELSTAR
FLEUMEUR-BODOU
ANDOVER

US 10c
Skylab

1984
NICARAGUA aéreo   C$4.00
1ra. FOTO CARA OCULTA DE LA LUNA

USA 18c
Benefiting Mankind

ПОЧТА СССР
НОВЫЙ ЭТАП КОСМИЧЕСКОЙ ЭРЫ
10к
ЗЕМЛЯ
ОКЕАН БУРЬ
ЛУНА
СТАРТ 31·1·1966   3·2·1966
МЯГКАЯ ПОСАДКА

"ЛУНА-9"-НА ЛУНЕ   СОВЕТСКАЯ ЛАБОРАТОРИЯ ДЕЙСТВУЕТ НА
10к
3·2·1966
ПОЧТА СССР
"ЛУНА-9"   ТЕЛЕСЕАНС С ЛУНЫ

ПОЧТА СССР
1991   20
СОВМЕСТНЫЙ КОСМИЧЕСКИЙ ПОЛЕТ
СССР - ВЕЛИКОБРИТАНИЯ
СССР
260591
КОСМОДРОМ БАЙКОНУР

ПОЧТА 1961
1 РУБЛЬ
XXII СЪЕЗД КПСС
СССР
СЛАВА КПСС!
СЛАВА СОВЕТСКОМУ НАРОДУ!

MONGOLIA
СССР
ЛУНИК II 13 IX 1959
25
МОНГОЛ ШУУДАН

10c
AIR MAIL
UNITED STATES
FIRST MAN ON THE MOON

DEVELOPING YOUR THEME

When you decide on a theme, it is a good idea to save every stamp that shows some aspect of the subject. As your collection grows, you will find that some stamps show the subject better than others. The less important stamps can then be swapped as your collection fills with better items.

Eventually, you will need to separate your stamps into different groups. There are two main ways of doing this:

SORTING STAMPS INTO DETAILED GROUPS

If you are collecting animals, then you may group the stamps of the class of animal shown, for example mammals, reptiles, or insects. Later, when your collection of mammals on stamps grows, you may decide to specialize in big cats, as on these stamps from Canada, Jersey, and Africa. This will give you plenty of opportunity to add extra stamps to a page without spoiling the design.

The disadvantage is that the collection can look very messy, because the stamps come from many countries and they may be of totally different shapes and sizes.

COLLECTING BY SETS

In this case, the aim is to include complete sets of stamps which show the theme, as in this set of architecture stamps from Singapore. The sets are kept together and individual stamps are not shown unless they show a particularly interesting feature not included in any set. The album is usually divided by country and the sets are displayed together in order. If one stamp is missing from a set, then a space is left for it to be added later.

This method creates a neat collection that looks more attractive than a willy-nilly mixture of stamps. Notes and features can still be included.

Puffins (above right) are among the best-loved of birds, not least because of their marvelous brightly colored bills. These examples are from France, Gibraltar, and Great Britain.

This set of stamps (right) features several birds found in the Seychelles. The set commemorates the Fourth Pan African Ornithological Congress.

The birds of tropical islands are among the most striking. These examples (far right) are from Antigua and Madagascar.

BIRDS EVERYWHERE

Birds are the most popular thematic subject, perhaps because they are attractive and almost every country has issued stamps with birds on them. Because there are so many stamps to choose from, you will probably need to specialize. To do this, you will need to learn more about the different species of birds. Try looking in books from the library or at wildlife programs on television.

A collection can be very simple and sorted by species. You may specialize in particular types of bird, such as ducks or parrots. Alternatively, special habitats can make an interesting collection. For example, look for stamps which show birds that live on cliffs or that nest on the ground. You can add information about the birds, but be careful not to include so much that the stamps themselves are lost.

PUFFINS

Ducks (below) are often found on stamps. These stamps from the U.S. and France illustrate ducks in flight. Once your collection of duck stamps grows, you might like to include other birds that live in wetlands, such as the grebe. This Falkland Islands stamp features the great grebe.

WETLAND BIRDS

BIRDS OF THE SEYCHELLES

ISLAND BIRDS

EVENTS AND FESTIVALS

There are stamps to mark the majority of important events, such as battles and revolutions, and political, royal, and sporting events. You can choose one or two of these special themes and build up your own stamp stories.

SWIFTER, HIGHER, STRONGER

Every two years, countries all over the world issue stamps to commemorate the Olympic Games. You could try to collect all the issues for one year, or a set from as many games as possible.

The modern Olympic Games were first held in Athens, Greece in 1896. A set of stamps was issued to commemorate the event.

The 1976 Olympics were held in Montreal, Canada. These Belgian stamps (left) were issued to commemorate the event. Four years later, the Olympics were held in Los Angeles, and Portugal issued this beautiful set (below).

The 24th Olympic Games in 1988 (right) prompted the issue of this set from the Solomon Islands.

Turkmenistan issued these stamps (below) to commemorate the 1992 Olympic Games.

Christmas stamps have been issued since 1898 (right). You could keep a scrapbook of Christmas stamps, together with Christmas cards you have received and a description of different Christmas customs around the world.

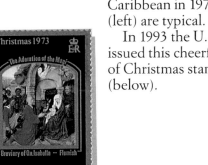

CHRISTMAS ALL OVER THE WORLD

Christmas is marked every year by an issue of commemorative stamps by almost all the countries of the world.

The small islands of the British Commonwealth often use Renaissance religious paintings for their Christmas issues. These sets issued by the Cook Islands in the Pacific Ocean in 1971 (right) and the Cayman Islands in the Caribbean in 1973 (left) are typical.

In 1993 the U.S. issued this cheerful set of Christmas stamps (below).

TRANSPORTATION THEMES

This stamp from the Philippines shows the sleek lines of a modern locomotive, with a volcano smoking dramatically in the background.

Transportation themes are very popular with stamp collectors: they feature three times on the top ten list. Luckily for collectors, many countries issue stamps on all aspects of transportation so you can specialize in any field you like.

TRAINS
Everything from early steam engines to modern high-speed trains are found on stamps. Some stamps have illustrated drawings showing all the details of a locomotive, others show the train in action, often with great billowing clouds of smoke. Your collection could show the history and development of engines and railways, or just a selection of individual trains.

Railways have always carried letters and packages – some even issued their own stamps (see pages 26–27). There are also several private railway companies that have their own stamps and special, colorful envelopes. If you visit a private railway, look for a souvenir to add to your collection.

This Japanese stamp shows a steam engine in all its glory, set against magnificent scenery.

This 1991 Danish stamp of a locomotive shows a lot of fine detail.

This 1979 Indian stamp is one of many demonstrating the importance of aircraft in delivering mail.

This 1977 stamp (above) from Antigua celebrates the 75th anniversary of the first flight by the Wright brothers by illustrating their biplane.

AIRCRAFT
Although the first manned flight was in 1903, flying did not become established until the 1920s. Only small planes were made at first, some of which were used to open new mail routes. There was little passenger travel until the 1930s, when planes carried between 20 and 30 passengers and were definitely not comfortable! Today, millions of people every year fly on jumbo jets that can carry over 500 people and fly nearly halfway around the world without refueling.

You can choose to collect stamps that feature certain types of aircraft, such as biplanes or jets, or certain uses of aircraft, such as military or civilian. Of course, aircraft have always played an important role in delivering mail. Airmail is essential for remote places, and planes are often featured on the stamps of such countries.

Military jets are displayed on this stamp from Australia (right), whereas the one from New Zealand (above left) shows a flying boat, and the one from the Philippines (below left) features a famous Filipino aviator in battle.

This pair of 1979 Canadian stamps features flying boats.

SHIPS

There are many different types of ship, from small yachts to huge ocean-going liners. You may want to confine your collection to one type from the start. You can collect small boats from around the world such as rowboats, sailboats, and fishing boats, or large vessels such as passenger ships and cruise liners.

Warships and submarines are not easy to find but can look spectacular, so keep an eye open for these.

Ships in full sail are always dramatic, as these French stamps from 1971 and 1975 show.

This Chinese stamp of 1946 (left) is unusual since it illustrates all three main forms of transportation: ship, aircraft, and train.

Stamps featuring submarines, like this 1982 South African one (below), are rare, so they should take a prominent place in your collection.

AUTOMOBILES AND TRUCKS

The first vehicle resembling the modern car was a steam-powered passenger-carrying vehicle built by Englishman Richard Trevithick in 1801. Since then, the internal combustion engine and the four-stroke engine have led to the mass production and use of cars all over the world.

Your collection could feature just one type of car, such as racing cars, or all the cars of one manufacturer, such as Mercedes-Benz.

Alternatively, you could feature steam-powered automobiles, or early gasoline-powered cars, or concentrate on modern sports cars. As in any theme, the choice is yours.

This 1984 pair of stamps from Afghanistan (above) features early gasoline-powered cars.

This Bulgarian stamp of 1986 shows a powerful modern racing car.

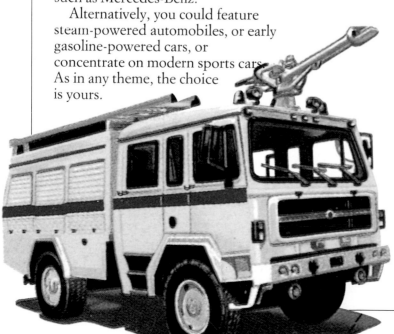

Unusual vehicles, like this yellow fire engine (left), make good subjects for a collection.

THEMES GALORE!

TEN WACKY STAMP THEMES

1 Bicycles
2 Cameras
3 Glass
4 Jazz
5 Left-handed People
6 Mustaches
7 Parachutes
8 Pyramids
9 Subways
10 Volcanoes

There is no end to the list of subjects that can be selected as themes for stamp collections. The choice of stamps and how they are displayed is entirely up to you. Adding notes on the history of a subject and other useful information will add interest to the collection. Here are just a few suggestions.

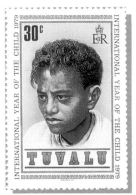

CHILDREN

Babies and children are popular subjects for stamps. Many stamps also show something about the countries where the children live. You might like to collect all the stamps of an omnibus issue, such as that for the International Year of the Child in 1979.

This set of stamps (above) was issued by Tuvalu, one of the Melanesian islands in the Pacific Ocean, to commemorate the International Year of the Child.

These two stamps (above) from Egypt commemorate Mother's Day in 1957 and 1962. Between 1958 and 1961, Egypt and Syria joined forces and were known as the United Arab Republic. After Syria left the union, Egypt retained United Arab Republic as its official name until 1971.

NURSING

There are numerous stamps that picture nurses. Your collection could concentrate on nurses' work and how it has changed over the years, or perhaps include famous nurses, such as Florence Nightingale and Clara Barton.

These three stamps show nurses at work. One (above left) was issued by Cyprus to commemorate the centenary of the International Red Cross. The U.S. stamp of 1981 (left) commemorates the centenary of the American Red Cross, founded by Clara Barton. As shown on this Turkish stamp (above), the emblem of the Red Cross in Muslim countries is a red crescent.

Both these stamps (above) illustrate the traditional image of the nurse as "the lady with the lamp." One was issued by Australia in 1955, the other by Korea in 1973.

FLAGS

One way to keep track of a country's history is to look for flags on stamps. These often change when a country becomes independent and changes its name. Also, organizations such as the United Nations, the European Community, and the Red Cross have flags that are sometimes featured on the stamps of member countries.

COSTUMES

There are lots of stamps showing people wearing special costumes. Some sets show national costumes and others show people wearing interesting or unusual clothes that happen to be in fashion. Look for stamps showing old paintings with people in historical costumes. This will add variety to your collection.

EXPLORERS

Explorers are featured on the stamps of many nations. An interesting collection can be made with maps and notes showing their routes and any special discoveries they made.

FLOWERS

Flowers are a popular theme. You can decide to collect one species, such as roses or orchids, or all the flowers of one country.

This New Zealand definitive shows the beautiful Diamond Jubilee rose.

MARINE LIFE

Marine life is a wonderfully varied theme. Seven-tenths of the earth's surface is covered by water, and many stamps and sets depict fish of all kinds, whales, sea plants, and coral reefs.

This Jamaican stamp shows a pair of beautiful whales.

The dramatic red fire fish on this stamp from the Tokelau Islands is typical of those found among the coral reefs of the Pacific Ocean.

These stunning composite stamps (right) from Malaysia (below right) feature three examples of plant life growing on coral reefs, whereas the beautiful miniature sheet (right) shows the coral growing on the reef.

MAPS

Stamps showing maps can be an interesting addition to a thematic collection on one country, or to a project on either history or exploration.

This Swedish stamp shows a map of Stockholm, the Swedish capital. The stamps from Fiji show an aerial view of the islands and their position in the Pacific Ocean.

FISHING

You can collect stamps showing fishing as a sport or as a commercial activity. You may decide to include fishing as a secondary topic in your collection on fish. You might like to look for stamps showing trawlermen as those stamps are usually full of action.

An Icelandic trawler.

SHOW OFF YOUR STAMPS

All dedicated stamp collectors want their stamps to look their best. There are many ways in which stamps may be displayed in school projects and scrapbooks as well as in stamp collections. You might like to include project pages in your album or make up posters that you can display on your wall.

Stamps are very useful for illustrating projects because they mark so many important events – battles, revolutions, royal anniversaries, great discoveries, scientific inventions, famous people, and so on.

For instance, a project on Antarctica could include stamps showing the wildlife, geography, and history of the continent, the people who have explored it, their means of transportation, and equipment.

The possibilities are endless – the pages in this section just give you some suggestions and tips.

Many countries have produced stamps illustrating the magnificent scenery and amazing wildlife of Antarctica. These stamps, along with pictures, maps, and other information, could form the basis of a fascinating project on Antarctica.

PROJECTS AND DISPLAYS

You might be asked to do a project at school and want to illustrate your work with examples from your stamp collection. All over the world, stamps are used to teach or remind people about everyday facts, such as health, road safety, and the environment, so you should be able to find a stamp to illustrate almost any topic. Here are some examples of stamps used to inform people.

SMOKING KILLS!
This set of two stamps from Saudi Arabia (above) warns that smoking is dangerous to health.

DRUG AND ALCOHOL ABUSE
This striking 1973 stamp from Austria (above) shows the dangers of drug abuse. The U.S. stamp (left) encourages alcoholics to stop drinking.

ROAD SAFETY
Stamps make colorful illustrations in a project on road safety. These stamps from Switzerland and Australia remind people to be careful whether walking or riding a bicycle on the road.

MAKING A DISPLAY

You might want to make a display for your project. Here are a few tips to help make your display a success.

WHAT YOU NEED

- Mounting board or stiff paper
- Scissors
- Pencil, ruler, and eraser for planning
- Plastic stamp mounts
- Photo corners for covers or cards
- Glue or paste for paper additions to collages
- Tracing paper to copy maps or other drawings
- Pen for writing neat notes and outlining
- Colored pens or pencils for drawing
- Thumbtacks for hanging

PLANNING
- Make a rough drawing of how the finished display should look.
- Make sure your stamps are highlighted as the important feature of the display.

BUILDING THE DISPLAY
- Start with the biggest items.
- Use photo corners to put postcards or covers on the boards.
- Stick the mounts in position before putting in the stamps.

WRITING NOTES AND ADDING DRAWINGS
- Write notes on clean paper, cut them out neatly, and glue them in position on the board.
- Draw pictures on paper, cut them out, and glue them down.

ADDING THE FINISHING TOUCHES
- Underline headings using a ruler and fine pen and draw neat lines linking stamps with maps and pictures.

COMPETITIONS

Your local stamp club probably runs annual competitions with a junior section. Competition entries will be displayed on competition day, and judged by experienced collectors.

To enter a competition, find out what categories are available and decide whether any part of your collection is suitable. Make sure you understand the competition rules and how the entries are marked.

Judges look for neat presentation, an interesting display, and well-chosen stamps. The information, maps, or drawings that explain the stamps are important features on a competition entry.

Allow plenty of time to prepare your entry. Colored drawings and notes must show details about the stamps or the collection, so it takes a lot of thought to plan an entry that will win!

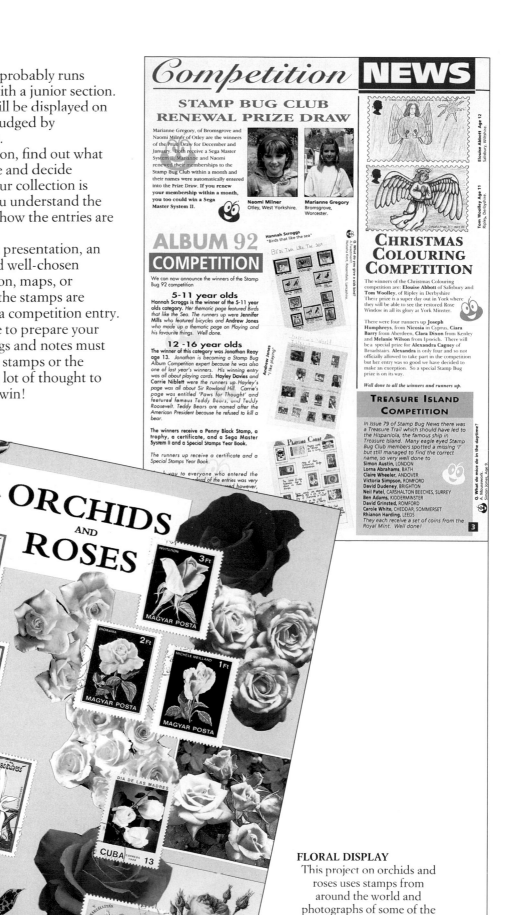

FLORAL DISPLAY
This project on orchids and roses uses stamps from around the world and photographs of some of the most beautiful species to create an attractive display.

POSTERS AND SCRAPBOOKS

The best way to make the most of stamp collecting is to do lots of different and decorative things with your stamps. If you have only a few stamps, try making a striking poster to put on your wall. You could hang small cards of stamps on a mobile, or make a stand-up card, like a birthday card, to display some of your stamps. You are sure to enjoy making up imaginative ways of using stamps.

Besides the stamps themselves, you can include magazine clippings, greetings cards, calendars, postcards, and photographs. Make sure the extras don't crowd out your stamps, though!

SAVE THE WORLD
This poster uses stamps from all over the world to illustrate the importance of conserving plants and wildlife, and taking care of our planet.

Phonecards are collected in many countries. They can make an interesting feature on a poster, like these British ones depicting an owl and a heron, or this Australian one of the Barossa Valley vineyards.

SCRAPBOOKS
Keeping a scrapbook is always fun, and you might enjoy your stamps even more if you keep some of them this way. For instance, you could keep your album for your main collection and put special items like a collection of cinderellas (see pages 36–37) in your scrapbook.

You could keep a scrapbook of your vacation, including photographs and postcards. Keep tickets, catalogues or programs, or a special souvenir.

Using a Maxicard, such as this one of a Welsh pony, is a good way to show the detail of a stamp on a poster.

STAMP BOOKLETS

Booklets were first introduced in 1900 as a good way of selling a small number of stamps together.

The first booklet machines were introduced in 1936. These machines are found at post offices and in stores.

At first booklets were stitched or stapled at one side. Special sheets of stamps had to be printed that had the panes of stamps facing different ways. The name for stamps printed this way is tête-bêche. Stamps in booklets are often imperforate on their outer edges.

Most modern booklets have cardboard covers with one pane of stamps inside, fixed to the card by their margin. These are called folded booklets and were first introduced in Sweden. Booklet covers are often attractive with notes on the stamps inside so that they look good and add interest to a thematic collection.

COUNTRY NAMES

Great Britain is the only country that does not put its name on the stamps it issues. All other stamps include the name of the country in the design. This name will be written in the language of the nation, so sometimes this may be in a different alphabet from the one you know. The country name may also be shortened and this can make it difficult to identify, too.

The name Lao, the map, and the postmark that shows part of Vientiane, the capital city, help to identify this stamp as from Laos.

Warszawskie is written down the side of this stamp, which is a clue since Warsaw is the capital of Poland.

▌ Find the name on the stamp. Write it down, making sure you copy it exactly. Then you can compare your note instead of handling the stamp too much.

▌ If there is a postmark on the stamp, then try to read the name of the town. This is when it is useful to have the stamp on the envelope. Write down the town name, then check it against a world atlas.

▌ Sometimes the picture on the stamp helps to narrow the choice of countries.

▌ Look for other features which may give away the country, such as a flag, the language used, or the currency used.

The list of country names on the opposite page will help to identify most of the foreign stamps in your collection. Occasionally, you may come across a batch of old stamps that do not have country names. These stamps were printed before 1873 when the rule was made that every country except Great Britain had to have its name on its stamps. These stamps may be difficult to identify so look for clues in the design to help you.

If you have a very unusual stamp and you cannot find the country name in the list, here are a few ideas to follow.

Chinese stamps always feature this symbol, which is the Chinese character for China.

NAMES OF COUNTRIES USING A–Z ALPHABET

Name on stamp	English translation
Afghanes	Afghanistan
Arabie Sauodite	Saudi Arabia
Bayern	Bavaria (German state)
Belgie or Belgique	Belgium
Braunschweig	Brunswick (German state)
Cambodge	Cambodia
CCCP	Union of Socialist Soviet Republics (or the Soviet Union)
Centrafricaine	Central African Republic
Ceskoslovensko	Czechoslovakia
Danmark	Denmark
DDR	East Germany
Deutsche Bundepost	West Germany until 1990, Germany thereafter
Deutsche Bundepost Berlin	West Berlin
Deutsche Post or Reich	Germany
Dominicana	Dominican Republic
Eesti	Estonia
Egypte or Egyptienne	Egypt
Eire	Ireland (Republic)
España or Española	Spain
Forøyar	Faroe Islands
Française	France
Grønland	Greenland
Helvetia	Switzerland
Italia	Italy
Jugoslavia	Yugoslavia
Kibris	Cyprus
KSA	Saudi Arabia
Lao	Laos
LAR	Libya
Liban or Libanaise	Lebanon
Magyar Posta	Hungary
Maroc	Morocco
Nippon	Japan
Norge	Norway
Osterreich	Austria
Persanes	Iran
Pilipinas	Phillipines
Polska	Poland
Pulau Pinang	Penang (Malayan state)
Reichspost	Germany
RF	France
Romana	Romania
RSA	South Africa
Rwandaise	Rwanda
SA	Saudi Arabia
Sachsen	Saxony (German state)
Salvador	El Salvador
Shqiperia (and similar)	Albania
Siam	Thailand
Suid Afrika	South Africa
Suidwes Afrika	South West Africa
Suomi	Finland
Sverige	Sweden
SWA	South West Africa
Tchad	Chad
Toga	Tonga
Togolaise	Togo
Turkiye	Turkey
UAE	United Arab Emirates
UAR	United Arab Republic (Egypt and Syria 1958–61, Egypt 1961–71)
USA	United States of America
Vaticane	Vatican City
Viet-nam Cong-Hoa	South Vietnam
Viet-nam Dan Chu Cong Hoa	North Vietnam
YAR	Yemen Arab Republic
Z. Afr. Republiek	Transvaal (South African state)

These stamps are postmarked Luzern, a city in Switzerland.

DDR stands for Deutsche Democratische Republik, or German Democratic Republic, the name for the former East Germany.

Hellas is the Greek name for Greece. It is sometimes shown as ELLAS.

OLD AND NEW COUNTRY NAMES

Here is a list of some of the most important name changes that you may notice on stamps.

Old Name	New Name (and date of independence)
Aden	South Arabian Federation (1965)
Basutoland	Lesotho (1966)
Bechuanaland	Botswana (1966)
British East Africa	Kenya, Uganda and Tanganyika (1903)
British Guiana	Guyana (1966)
British Honduras	Belize (1973)
Burma	Myanmar (1991)
Cambodia	Kampuchea (1980)
Ceylon	Sri Lanka (1972)
Congo	Zaire (1971)
Ellice Islands	Tuvalu (1976)
Gilbert Islands	Kiribati (1979)
Gold Coast	Ghana (1957)
New Hebrides	Vanuatu (1980)
North Borneo	Sabah (1964)
Nyasaland	Malawi (1964)
Persia	Iran (1935)
Rhodesia (Northern)	Zambia (1964)
Rhodesia (Southern)	Zimbabwe (1978)
Siam	Thailand (1949)
South West Africa	Namibia (1968)
Tanganyika	Tanzania (1965)
Zanzibar	Tanzania (1965)

GLOSSARY

Aerogram A sheet of thin paper with a stamp printed on it. This can be mailed to any foreign country. The paper is usually blue and the sheet folds twice before it is sealed on three sides.

Airmail An envelope that has been carried on most of its journey by airplane. Most of these envelopes have a blue label that reads By Air Mail/Par Avion.

Approvals These are stamps sent out by mail from a dealer to sell to collectors. The stamps are sent in a small approvals book and each one is individually priced. You pay for the stamps that you keep and return the rest to the dealer.

Bisect This is a stamp that has been cut in half and used in the mail. Occasionally in the past, post offices ran out of stamps of a particular value. One way to allow the correct postage to be paid was to cut in half stamps of twice the value. Bisected stamps are valuable when used on covers but only when the Post Office allowed this to happen when there was a shortage. (*See* **Provisional**.)

Blind Perforations This problem has existed for years. It occurs when the perforating pin fails to cut the paper completely and the round piece of paper that was supposed to be cut out remains in place.

Block A block is the name given to four or more stamps joined together in their original shape. It is often better to keep stamps together in a block, especially if they are old stamps. Do not be worried about splitting blocks of modern stamps as they are not worth any more than separate stamps unless the block has a special marking or variety.

Booklet For convenience stamps are also sold in small booklets. The earlier booklets had panes of four or six stamps stapled or sewn together. Modern booklets have a cardboard cover with a block of stamps stuck in by their margin.

Cachet This mark on a cover includes an inscription. Most cachets today are printed on the envelope rather than applied by rubber stamp.

Catalogue A book which lists stamps and gives the publisher's selling price for each stamp (*see pages 56–57*).

Charity Stamps Sometimes Post Offices produce stamps that cost more than the amount indicated for postage. The additional cost of the stamp is donated to a charity. Some countries, such as New Zealand and Switzerland, issue charity stamps each year.

Cinderellas This is the term given to stamps that are not used in the ordinary mail. They include local stamps and revenue stamps.

Circular Date Stamp (cds) A small, circular postmark that gives the Post Office name and the date. These are the neatest postmarks.

Classic Classic stamps are the very first stamps that were issued. Generally, the "classic period" of stamps extends to about 1870.

Coil A coil is a long roll of stamps made to be sold in a vending machine.

Color Changeling Color changelings can be the result of a number of chemicals, as well as water and strong light. The colors are sometimes made fraudulently in order to create rare colors on stamps.

Color Trial When stamps were printed in only one or two colors it was quite common to try a series of different colors or different shades of the same color before deciding on the color to print a stamp. The sample stamps in different colors or shades are known as color trials.

Commemorative These are stamps which are designed specifically to mark an anniversary or special event.

Cover This is an envelope with stamps that has been through the mail. Some collectors stick stamps on envelopes, then mail them to their own address so that they can put them in their collections. These are called philatelic covers. Covers that have been used by companies for business are sometimes called commercial covers. Generally, commercial covers are more interesting to collect than envelopes that have been especially prepared by a stamp collector.

Definitive These are everyday stamps, readily available from the post office. Usually they are small and depict the leader of the country. They must cover all postal rates, so their face values range from the smallest currency unit to high values for use on heavy packages.

Die When a printing plate for a stamp is made with the design either raised (typographed) or cut into the surface (recessed), then the picture is cut or scratched out by hand. This is known as the master die and it is used to make the shape for each stamp on the printing plate.

Doctor Blade In photogravure printing, the surplus ink is removed from the printing plate by a knife or blade. This is called the doctor blade. If the printing suddenly stops the doctor blade leaves a long mark across the paper. The stamps are usually printed sideways so this line runs down the sheet. (*See pages 22–23*).

Dry Print This is a variety caused when the printing ink runs out or does not flow properly. The ink becomes faint and sometimes it may be missing completely. This effect may only appear over a few rows of stamps before being corrected.

Essay Any piece of artwork made by the designer of a stamp is called an essay. Sometimes printers produce trials or samples of stamps that are not chosen and these are also called essays.

First Day Cover For every new issue the Post Office produces special envelopes with an illustration. On the day of issue, or first day, the new stamps are stuck on the envelopes and mailed. There are special boxes to mail first day covers so that the stamps will be carefully canceled by hand, often with a special postmark.

Franking This describes the stamps on the envelope and is usually the cost of the postage. For example, a letter with a 4-cent stamp and a 10-cent stamp would have a 14-cent franking.

Gutter Margin When a sheet of stamps is made up of two or more panes of stamps, the blank strip between them is called the gutter margin. The old term for this is *interpanneau* (between panes) margin.

Imperforate This is a stamp without perforations. The first stamps were made before perforations were invented. Modern stamps may be imperforate if the perforating machine breaks down.

Issue Another name for a set of stamps. It is often used to describe a definitive set that is identified by the date of issue or watermark.

Joins The paper that stamps are printed on may be joined for two reasons:
- When the roll of paper runs out during printing, the printing presses are stopped and a new roll put on. The two rolls are joined together by sticking the old one to the new one, usually by the glue on the back of the paper. The printers should throw these joined stamps away but some pass through unnoticed.
- Some coils are made by joining together rows of stamps from ordinary sheets. These are called coil joins.

Kiloware Some stamps are sold still stuck on bits of envelope. They are tied in plastic bags and sold by weight.

Maxicard This is a picture postcard with a stamp relating to the subject of the card affixed to the picture side of the card and postmarked.

Meter Mail Instead of using stamps, many companies now have machines that print the value of the postage on the envelope, or on a slip of paper that is stuck on the envelope.

The meter in the machine is pre-set with postage credit by a postal worker. The meter counts down the postage and stops working when the credit has been used up.

Miniature Sheet Sometimes a new set of stamps is printed together in a small sheet including one stamp of each value. Occasionally a single stamp is specially printed in a sheet of its own with large margins all round. These are called miniature sheets.

Mint A stamp is said to be mint if it has not been through the mail and still has its original glue on the back. A stamp is "unmounted mint (u/m)" if the stamp has never been hinged and the gum is completely unspoiled.

Offset on Reverse If the ink is still wet when new sheets of stamps are stacked together, part of the design is transferred to the glue of the sheets above. It appears as a mirror image of the proper design. When this happens the printing is said to be offset on reverse or set-off. This occasionally happened in older printing methods when sheets were printed one at a time but it is almost unknown with modern printing presses.

Omnibus When a special event is commemorated on the stamps of many different countries this is called an omnibus issue. This term is sometimes used when all the sets have a similar design.

Overprint A message may be printed on a stamp. It may be used instead of printing special stamps to commemorate a special event.

Pane A pane of stamps is a block with margins all around. There may be more than one pane in a sheet. The stamps in booklets usually only have one margin where the stamps are held in place; these are called booklet panes.

Perfin Some stamps have sets of tiny holes in the middle of them. These often make a series of letters and were punched by companies to make sure that their stamps were only used on business letters.

Philately This is the name given to the study of postage stamps and postal history. Philatelists are people who take their collecting seriously and study the history of their stamps in great detail. Often, a philatelist has a small collection with lots of information about each stamp.

Phosphor Bands These bands, or lines, glow slightly when exposed to ultra-violet light. They were printed on top of stamps so that automatic sorting machines turned letters the right way, making the address easy to read. Today the phosphor is included in the paper when it is made.

Plate This refers to the printing plate. Each printing plate is given its own number. This is usually printed in the margin of the sheet although some stamps used to have the plate number included in the design.

Plate Number Each printing cylinder is given a number that is printed in the margin of the sheet of stamps. When one printing cylinder becomes worn or damaged it is replaced by the printer and a new number will be used. When stamps are printed in more than one color, a series of numbers will be found in the sheet margin. The numbers are usually printed near a corner of the sheet. A corner block of stamps that includes the numbers is called a cylinder block.

Postage Due When a letter is put in the mail without enough stamps on it the Post Office charges the person who receives the letter. Special stamps are put on the envelope to show the amount to be paid. These stamps have the words "postage due" (or the foreign equivalent) incorporated in the design.

Postal History Postal history is the study of postal rates and of the routing of mail.

Postal Stationery Post offices sell envelopes and cards with the postage printed on them. These are called postal stationery.

Precancel A few countries sell stamps that are overprinted with a mark that looks like a postmark. These are used on vast quantities of letters that are mailed at a reduced rate.

Presentation Pack Many countries sell sets of new stamps in special display packs. There is an illustration on the front and a lot of information about the issue inside.

Proof This is a sample produced by the printers for approval before all the stamps are printed.

Provisional During the last century, when many European countries were responsible for the administration of colonies, stamps were printed in the mother country. When stocks ran low the colonies would order a new batch of stamps. However, communications and transportation were slow and haphazard, and occasionally the stamps of one value ran out completely before the new supply arrived. A provisional issue would then be made. This would usually be another stamp overprinted with the required value, but sometimes a completely new stamp would be made locally.

Remainders In the past, when some countries stopped using a stamp, they sold all the leftover stock to dealers at a discount. The stamps were canceled first, so that they could only be used by collectors. Some of these cancels are distinctive and the stamps are described as having remainder cancels.

Reprint It was many years after stamps were first used before stamp collecting became popular, so early stamps were not always saved. Later, when stamp collectors were looking for older stamps, some countries were so overwhelmed with requests that they got the old printing plates and printed new examples of earlier stamps. These reprints are worth a lot less than the original stamps, so don't get too excited if you think that you have found an early rarity. Most reprints were made between 1860 and 1880. They tend to be in brighter colors and on thicker paper than the originals.

Se tenant This refers to two stamps of different designs joined together.

Set A set is a group of stamps that go together. Most sets have a common theme. Some definitive sets may have extra values added to them over the years. Catalogues list a range of dates from when the first stamps were issued to the latest additions.

Space-filler This is an expensive stamp that is not in very good condition but fills a space in a collection until a better example is available or can be afforded.

Special These stamps are larger than normal, and depict scenes from the life of a country.

Specimen Some stamps are found overprinted with the word "SPECIMEN." Traditionally, these are stamps sent to head post offices around the world to let them know about the stamps that have been issued.

Surcharge This is a stamp with an overprint of a different value to the stamp. These were made when the Post Office ran out of one value.

Tête-bêche This refers to two stamps joined together with one printed upside down to the other.

Traffic Lights Modern stamps are printed in many different colours. As well as printing cylinder numbers in the sheet margin the printers often print coloured dots to show the colour of the ink. The first multicoloured stamps were printed in three colours and the three coloured dots looked a little like a set of traffic lights.

Used Abroad During the last century many of the richer nations had post offices in foreign countries. These foreign post offices used the postage stamps of their own nation and had their own postmarks. Stamps with these postmarks are called Used Abroad.

Vignette This is a label stuck on an envelope that usually advertises an event.

INDEX

FL 33782
JUN
98

RG. FL

M

337

28

JUN

98